Voices from the
RAILWAYS

Voices from the
RAILWAYS

*How the railways
changed our lives*

Foreword by Peter Snow

EDITED BY

JULIAN HOLLAND

Published by AA Publishing (a trading name of AA Media Limited, whose registered office is Fanum House, Basingstoke, Hampshire RG21 4EA. Registered number 06112600).

First published in 2013.

10 9 8 7 6 5 4 3 2 1

Extracts from the journal of R W Carr, © 2007 Don Bramley.
Tom Rolt's letter, © reserved by The Talyllyn Railway Company.
Extracts from the interview with Richard Spendlove MBE, © 2010 Adrian Peel.
Interviews with Lawrie Inman, John Woodall, Stan Knowles and Dick Smith, © Poppleton History Society and the named individuals.
Interviews with Charles Day, William Squibb, Violet Lee, Betty Chalmers, Brian Palfreyman, Sidney Sheldrick, Mohammed Ayub, David Crew, Brian Connorton, Charles Cook, Stewart Currie, Colin Mellish, Bill Addy, Geoff Page, Christine McMillan, Trevor Adams, Ann Henderson, Catherine Gregory and Brian Druce were sourced from the National Archive of Railway Oral History, © National Railway Museum, York.

For a full list of permissions, sources and acknowledgements see pages 218–224.

Researched by Dr Susan Martin
Jacket design by Two Associates
Typeset by Austin Taylor and Tracey Butler
Printed and bound in the UK by Clays Ltd

A04983

Our books carrying the FSC label are printed on FSC certified paper. FSC is the only forest certification scheme endorsed by the leading environmental organisations.

MIX
Paper from responsible sources
FSC
www.fsc.org   FSC® C018072

Visit AA Publishing at theAA.com/shop

CONTENTS

SIGNIFICANT EVENTS ✦ 1900–1948

END OF AN ERA ✦ 1948–1968

NEW BEGINNINGS ✦ 1968–1990s

FOREWORD

IF, LIKE ME, you are already addicted to the thrill and enchantment of railways, you will not be able to put this book down. If you are not, lie back and allow yourself to be seduced. It is a magical trawl though the best, and some of the most eccentric, memories of the ongoing revolution that George Stephenson launched nearly two centuries ago. I say 'ongoing' because I believe that the train is once again being recognized as the fastest, safest and most comfortable way to travel. I used to fly to Manchester, Newcastle, Brussels and Paris. Now I get there faster by rail, and it may not be long before high-speed trains will make that true of Scotland too. This book tells us that in 1825 Stephenson himself dreamed of the day 'when railways will come to supersede almost all other forms of transport'. He was right – for a time – till aircraft and the motorway took over and Dr Beeching wielded his axe. But now Britain's travellers, exasperated by airport delays and clogged roads, are rediscovering the railways. And this book reminds us of the joys and the sheer romance of travelling by train. The actress Fanny Kemble writes in 1830 of how she travelled, wide-eyed, on the first steam train – 'the magical machine, with its flying white breath and rhythmical unvarying pace'.

From then on the mystique of the great age of steam takes over. There are some grumblers like William Wordsworth, who deplores the number of tourists being carried by train into the Lake District. There's the old snob who hates having to 'do with porters who never touch their hats'. But for most people who tell their stories in this book the railways are a source of fun and fascination: the signalman who thought he was free to leave his signal box and do some shooting in nearby fields, but was horrified to return and find a train full of holidaymakers impatiently waiting for the green light; the army officer who missed his train and managed to persuade a driver to stoke up his engine and give him a private lift; the fireman who was asked not to make a noise while shovelling coal and firing the engine for the overnight warming of the Royal Train. One tale that makes me laugh is the account of the passengers who, before the days of alarms or communication cords, had to haul themselves onto the roof of the train to attract the train driver's attention when their carriage caught fire.

I have stood for hours on busy British bridges watching express trains whistle past. I've watched the mighty steam locomotives that still pull passenger trains in Poland, and counted the scores of wagons that a Canadian Pacific engine drags through the Rockies. I've got the mandatory model railway that every railway enthusiast has in the loft at home. But none of this has provided me with the colour and vibrancy of railway life – stories that only people can tell – like the tales so aptly chosen and assembled by Julian Holland.

PETER SNOW
JANUARY 2013

INTRODUCTION

THE EARLY 19TH CENTURY saw Britain at the cutting edge of a transport revolution that changed the world forever. Plentiful supplies of coal, inventive minds and Victorian entrepreneurship powered an Industrial Revolution that made Britain the workshop of the world and laid the foundations for a global empire. The key to this success lay in the development of railways that by the mid-19th century were spreading their tentacles to all corners of the land. For the next 100 years continuous technological developments kept Britain at the forefront of railway transport that culminated in the golden age of high-speed luxury train travel of the 1930s. The austerity years that followed brought nationalisation and contraction and saw Britain's railways fighting for survival in a new age of road transport. By the skin of their teeth they survived and today they play an important role in keeping Britain on the move.

While the history of our railways is extremely well documented, the personal stories from the men and women who worked and travelled on them and whose lives were affected by them are less well known. To fill this void, this book pieces together a collection of first-hand accounts of life, work and travel on our railways from the 1820s to the end of the 20th century. It is a unique insight into the lives and times of Britain's much-loved railways.

The first chapter of this book includes accounts of a personal meeting with George Stephenson, the opening day of the Liverpool & Manchester Railway and the ups and downs of early rail travel. Landowners, farmers and even a Master at Eton School have their say about this new phenomenon that was about to transform their lives forever.

The accelerating growth of railways during the second half of the 19th century opened up Britain to millions of Victorians for the first time – personal accounts of trips to the Great Exhibition, the big cities, the countryside and the seaside vividly bring this to life. The railway workers are not forgotten either, with reports of driving locomotives, from royal trains to the humble shunter.

The early years of the 20th century saw Britain's railways reach their zenith, but the clouds of war were gathering. Personal descriptions of railway trips to the Continent are coupled with tales of political unrest, but the railways at home kept on running – workers in railway factories, railway guards along with drivers and fireman who had miraculous escapes from runaway trains all tell their stories. The First World War saw Government control of Britain's strategically important railways – personal accounts come from railway workers and journalists who witnessed the procession of troop and ambulance trains.

The war took its toll on the overworked Government-controlled railways, which survived only by amalgamating into four big companies in 1923 – the age of the super railway had arrived. This period begins with stories of undergraduates who worked on the railways during the 1926 General Strike, a trip on a bucolic Scottish branch line and the work of a railway canvasser. Then war again. The railways were stretched to the limit during the Second World War and here we can read vivid first-hand accounts of air raids, bomb damage, Winston Churchill's private train, evacuee trains and local defence volunteer corps who guarded against enemy sabotage. The vital work of women on the railways is not forgotten either, with tales from a passenger guard and a switchboard operator who witnessed the Luftwaffe raid on York station in 1942.

The end of the war saw austerity Britain on its knees. The big freeze of 1947 brought heroic tales from railwaymen while another railway phenomenon – train spotting – gathered pace with schoolboys. The dawn of 1948 saw Britain's crumbling railways nationalised, ushering in the era of British Railways, and here we have many personal accounts from a relatively recent period – now looked on with some nostalgia. A station master's family, locomotive cleaner, Kashmiri guard in Scotland, Yorkshire locomotive fireman, a Leeds' shunter, a postman on a Travelling Post Office all tell their stories while the effects of snow and floods and the Beeching closures also have their place. Deliberately crashing a train on a film set, accompanying race horses on train journeys and unloading circus trains complete the picture.

Voices from the Railways ends its fascinating journey through the life of Britain's railways with stories from a partially sighted typist who worked at Paddington station, a manager at Waterloo station, a female engine driver in Scotland, a bored clerk working in the ticket office at St Pancras and the everyday story of a man who changed his career in his late fifties to become a signalman in Worcestershire. Every bit of it is fascinating stuff!

JULIAN HOLLAND

EARLY STEAM

1825–1851

Abundant supplies of indigenous coal, inventive minds and entrepreneurial spirit were at the heart of Britain's Industrial Revolution. By 1825 the early steam locomotives of William Hedley and Timothy Hackworth had already proved their superiority to horsepower in hauling coal along iron tracks from collieries to industrial centres. In that year the Stockton & Darlington Railway was opened amidst great fanfare – engineered by George Stephenson and using his 'Locomotion No. 1', it was the world's first publicly subscribed railway.

Stephenson's ground-breaking 'Rocket' locomotive of 1829 and the opening of the world's first inter-city railway between Liverpool and Manchester in 1830 were just the beginning of a worldwide railway revolution. Built by thousands of 'navvies', Robert Stephenson's epic construction of the London & Birmingham Railway and Isambard Kingdom Brunel's high-speed broad-gauge Great Western Railway were soon to follow. Despite opposition from canal companies, the landed gentry and doom-mongers, by the mid-1840s around 7,000 miles of railways had been authorised by Parliament.

Despite the boom-and-bust cycle of 'Railway Mania', Britain's railway network continued to expand, albeit at a slower rate, and by the mid-19th century its tentacles were spreading around the land. Not only were a vast amount of raw materials and finished goods being carried, fuelling Britain's growth as the world's most powerful and richest nation, but also a new breed of travelling public – for the first time, the new working classes could leave behind the industrial squalor for a day trip to the seaside or countryside.

THE FUTURE OF RAILWAYS

GEORGE STEPHENSON ✦ 1825

*The 'Father of Railways' outlines his vision for
the future of this new form of transportation*

I THINK YOU will live to see the day, though I may not live so
long, when railways will come to supersede almost all other
methods of conveyance in this country, when mail coaches will
go by railway, and railroads will become the Great Highway for
the king and all his subjects. The time is coming when it will be
cheaper for a working man to travel on a railway than to walk on
foot. I know there are great and almost insurmountable
difficulties that will have to be encountered; but what I have said
will come to pass as sure as we live. I only wish I may live to see
the day, though that I can scarcely hope for, as I know how slow
all human progress is, and with what difficulty I have been able
to get the locomotive adopted...

EXTOLLING GEORGE STEPHENSON

FANNY KEMBLE ✦ 1830

*A popular young actress is entranced by her first train
ride and her meeting with George Stephenson*

Liverpool, 26th August 1830

MY DEAR H—,

A common sheet of paper is enough for love, but a foolscap
extra can alone contain a railroad and my ecstasies. There was
once a man, who was born at Newcastle-upon-Tyne, who was a
common coal-digger; this man had an immense constructiveness,

which displayed itself in pulling his watch to pieces and putting it together again; in making a pair of shoes when he happened to be some days without occupation; finally – here there is a great gap in my story – it brought him in the capacity of an engineer before a committee of the House of Commons, with his head full of plans for constructing a railroad from Liverpool to Manchester. It so happened that to the quickest and most powerful perceptions and conceptions, to the most indefatigable industry and perseverance, and the most accurate knowledge of the phenomena of nature as they affect his peculiar labours, this man joined an utter want of the 'gift of the gab'; he could no more explain to others what he meant to do and how he meant to do it, than he could fly; and therefore the members of the House of Commons, after saying, 'There is rock to be excavated to a depth of more than sixty feet, there are embankments to be made nearly to the same height, there is a swamp of five miles in length to be traversed, in which if you drop an iron rod it sinks and disappears: how will you do all this?' and receiving no answer but a broad Northumbrian 'I can't tell you how I'll do it, but I can tell you *I will do it*,' dismissed Stephenson as a visionary. Having prevailed upon a company of Liverpool gentlemen to be less incredulous, and having raised funds for his great undertaking, in December of 1826 the first spade was struck into the ground.

And now I will give you an account of my yesterday's excursion. A party of sixteen persons was ushered, into a large court-yard, where, under cover, stood several carriages of a peculiar construction, one of which was prepared for our reception. It was a long-bodied vehicle with seats placed across it, back to back; the one we were in had six of these benches, and was a sort of uncovered *char à banc*. The wheels were placed upon two iron bands, which formed the road, and to which they are fitted, being so constructed as to slide along without any danger of hitching or becoming displaced, on the same principle as a

17

thing sliding on a concave groove. The carriage was set in motion
by a mere push, and, having received this impetus, rolled with us
down an inclined plane into a tunnel, which forms the entrance
to the railroad. This tunnel is four hundred yards long (I believe),
and will be lighted by gas. At the end of it we emerged from
darkness, and, the ground becoming level, we stopped. There is
another tunnel parallel with this, only much wider and longer,
for it extends from the place which we had now reached, and
where the steam-carriages start, and which is quite out of
Liverpool, the whole way under the town, to the docks. This
tunnel is for wagons and other heavy carriages; and as the
engines which are to draw the trains along the railroad do not
enter these tunnels, there is a large building at this entrance
which is to be inhabited by steam-engines of a stationary turn of
mind, and different constitution from the travelling ones, which
are to propel the trains through the tunnels to the terminus in the
town, without going out of their houses themselves. The length
of the tunnel parallel to the one we passed through is (I believe)
two thousand two hundred yards. I wonder if you are
understanding one word I am saying all this while!

We were introduced to the little engine which was to drag us
along the rails. She (for they make these curious little fire-horses
all mares) consisted of a boiler, a stove, a small platform, a bench,
and behind the bench a barrel containing enough water to
prevent her being thirsty for fifteen miles – the whole machine
not bigger than a common fire-engine. She goes upon two
wheels, which are her feet, and are moved by bright steel legs
called pistons; these are propelled by steam, and in proportion as
more steam is applied to the upper extremities (the hip-joints,
I suppose) of these pistons, the faster they move the wheels; and
when it is desirable to diminish the speed, the steam, which
unless suffered to escape would burst the boiler, evaporates
through a safety-valve into the air. The reins, bit, and bridle of

this wonderful beast is a small steel handle, which applies or withdraws the steam from its legs or pistons, so that a child might manage it. The coals, which are its oats, were under the bench, and there was a small glass tube affixed to the boiler, with water in it, which indicates by its fullness or emptiness when the creature wants water, which is immediately conveyed to it from its reservoirs. There is a chimney to the stove, but as they burn coke there is none of the dreadful black smoke which accompanies the progress of a steam vessel. This snorting little animal, which I felt rather inclined to pat, was then harnessed to our carriage, and, Mr Stephenson having taken me on the bench of the engine with him, we started at about ten miles an hour.

The steam-horse being ill adapted for going up and down hill, the road was kept at a certain level, and appeared sometimes to sink below the surface of the earth, and sometimes to rise above it. Almost at starting it was cut through the solid rock, which formed a wall on either side of it, about sixty feet high. You can't imagine how strange it seemed to be journeying on thus, without any visible cause of progress other than the magical machine, with its flying white breath and rhythmical, unvarying pace, between these rocky walls, which are already clothed with moss and ferns and grasses; and when I reflected that these great masses of stone had been cut asunder to allow our passage thus far below the surface of the earth, I felt as if no fairy tale was ever half so wonderful as what I saw. Bridges were thrown from side to side across the top of these cliffs, and the people looking down upon us from them seemed like pigmies standing in the sky. I must be more concise, though, or I shall want room.

We were to go only fifteen miles, that distance being sufficient to show the speed of the engine, and to take us on to the most beautiful and wonderful object on the road. After proceeding through this rocky defile, we presently found ourselves raised upon embankments ten or twelve feet high; we then came to a moss, or swamp, of considerable extent, on which no human foot could tread without sinking, and yet it bore the road which bore us. This had been the great stumbling-block in the minds of the committee of the House of Commons; but Mr Stephenson has succeeded in overcoming it. A foundation of hurdles, or, as he called it, basket-work, was thrown over the morass, and the interstices were filled with moss and other elastic matter. Upon this the clay and soil were laid down, and the road does float, for we passed over it at the rate of five and twenty miles an hour, and saw the stagnant swamp water trembling on the surface of the soil on either side of us. I hope you understand me. The embankment had gradually been rising higher and higher, and in one place, where the soil was not settled enough to form banks, Stephenson had constructed artificial ones of wood-work, over which the mounds of earth were heaped, for he said that though the wood-work would rot, before it did so the banks of earth which covered it would have been sufficiently consolidated to support the road.

We had now come fifteen miles, and stopped where the road traversed a wide and deep valley. Stephenson made me alight and led me down to the bottom of this ravine, over which, in order to keep his road level, he has thrown a magnificent viaduct of nine arches, the middle one of which is seventy feet high, through which we saw the whole of this beautiful little valley. It was lovely and wonderful beyond all words. He here told me many curious things respecting this ravine: how he believed the Mersey had once rolled through it; how the soil had proved so unfavourable for the foundation of his bridge that it was built upon piles, which had been driven into the earth to an enormous depth; how, while digging for a foundation, he had come to a tree bedded in the earth fourteen feet below the surface of the ground; how tides are caused, and how another flood might be caused; all of which I have remembered and noted down at much greater length than I can enter upon it here. He explained to me the whole construction of the steam-engine, and said he could soon make a famous engineer of me, which, considering the wonderful things he has achieved, I dare not say is impossible. His way of explaining himself is peculiar, but very striking, and I understood, without difficulty, all that he said to me.

We then rejoined the rest of the party, and the engine having received its supply of water, the carriage was placed behind it, for it cannot turn, and was set off at its utmost speed, thirty-five miles an hour, swifter than a bird flies (for they tried the experiment with a snipe). You cannot conceive what that sensation of cutting the air was; the motion is as smooth as possible, too. I could either have read or written; and as it was, I stood up, and with my bonnet off 'drank the air before me'. The wind, which was strong, or perhaps the force of our own thrusting against it, absolutely weighed my eyelids down ... When I closed my eyes this sensation of flying was quite delightful, and strange beyond description; yet, strange as it was, I had a perfect sense of security, and not the slightest fear. At one time, to exhibit the power of the engine, having met another steam-carriage which was unsupplied with water, Mr Stephenson caused it to be fastened in front of ours; moreover, a wagon laden with timber was also chained to us, and thus propelling the idle steam-engine, and dragging the loaded wagon which was beside it, and our own carriage full of people behind, this brave little she-dragon of ours flew on. Farther on she met three carts, which, being fastened in front of her, she pushed on before her without the slightest delay or difficulty; when I add that this pretty little creature can run with equal facility either backward or forward, I believe I have given you an account of all her capacities. ...

Four years have sufficed to bring this great undertaking to an end. The railroad will be opened upon the 15th of next month. The Duke of Wellington is coming down to be present on the occasion, and, I suppose, what with the thousands of spectators and the novelty of the spectacle, there will never have been a scene of more striking interest. The whole cost of the work (including the engines and carriages) will have been eight hundred and thirty thousand pounds; and it is already worth double that sum. The directors have kindly offered us three places for the opening, which is a great favour, for people are bidding almost anything for a place, I understand.

LIVERPOOL & MANCHESTER RAILWAY OPENING DAY

FANNY KEMBLE ✦ 1830

A month later, Miss Kemble attended the opening of the Liverpool & Manchester Railway

Manchester, 20th September 1830

MY DEAR H—,

You probably have by this time heard and read accounts of the opening of the railroad, and the fearful accident which occurred at it, for the papers are full of nothing else. The accident you mention *did occur*...

I will tell you something of the events on the 15th, as, though you may be acquainted with the circumstances of poor Mr Huskisson's death, none but an eyewitness of the whole scene can form a conception of it. I told you that we had had places given to us, and it was the main purpose of our returning from Birmingham to Manchester to be present at what promised to be one of the most striking events in the scientific annals of our country.

We started on Wednesday last, to the number of about eight hundred people, in carriages constructed as I before described to you. The most intense curiosity and excitement prevailed, and, though the weather was uncertain, enormous masses of densely packed people lined the road, shouting and waving hats and handkerchiefs as we flew by them. What with the sight and sound of these cheering multitudes and the tremendous velocity with which we were borne past them, my spirits rose to the true champagne height, and I never enjoyed anything so much as the first hour of our progress. I had been unluckily separated from my mother in the first distribution of places, but by an exchange of seats which she was enabled to make she rejoined me when I was at the height of my ecstasy, which was considerably damped by finding that she was frightened to death, and intent upon nothing but devising means of escaping from a situation which appeared to her to threaten with instant annihilation herself and all her travelling companions.

While I was chewing the cud of this disappointment, which was rather bitter, as I had expected her to be as delighted as myself with our excursion, a man flew by us, calling out through a speaking-trumpet to stop the engine, for that somebody in the directors' carriage had sustained an injury. We were all stopped accordingly, and presently a hundred voices were heard exclaiming that Mr Huskisson was killed; the confusion that ensued is indescribable: the calling out from carriage to carriage to ascertain the truth, the contrary reports which were sent back to us, the hundred questions eagerly uttered at once, and the repeated and urgent demands for surgical assistance, created a sudden turmoil that was quite sickening. At last we distinctly ascertained that the unfortunate man's thigh was broken. From Lady W—, who was in the duke's carriage, and within three yards of the spot where the accident happened, I had the following details, the horror of witnessing which we were spared through our situation behind the great carriage.

The engine had stopped to take in a supply of water, and several of the gentlemen in the directors' carriage had jumped out to look about them. Lord W——, Count Batthyany, Count Matuscenitz, and Mr Huskisson among the rest were standing talking in the middle of the road, when an engine on the other line, which was parading up and down merely to show its speed, was seen coming down upon them like lightning. The most active of those in peril sprang back into their seats: Lord W—— saved his life only by rushing behind the duke's carriage, and Count Matuscenitz had but just leaped into it, with the engine all but touching his heels as he did so; while poor Mr Huskisson, less active from the effects of age and ill health, bewildered, too, by the frantic cries of 'Stop the engine! Clear the track!' that resounded on all sides, completely lost his head, looked helplessly to the right and left, and was instantaneously prostrated by the fatal machine, which dashed down like a thunderbolt upon him, and passed over his leg, smashing and mangling it in the most horrible way. (Lady W—— said she distinctly heard the crushing of the bone.) So terrible was the effect of the appalling accident that, except that ghastly 'crushing' and poor Mrs Huskisson's piercing shriek, not a sound was heard or a word uttered among the immediate spectators of the catastrophe. Lord W—— was the first to raise the poor sufferer, and calling to aid his surgical skill, which is considerable, he tied up the severed artery, and for a time, at least, prevented death by loss of blood. Mr Huskisson was then placed in a carriage with his wife and Lord W——, and the engine, having been detached from the directors' carriage, conveyed them to Manchester.

So great was the shock produced upon the whole party by this event, that the Duke of Wellington declared his intention not to proceed, but to return immediately to Liverpool. However, upon its being represented to him that the whole population of Manchester had turned out to witness the procession, and that a disappointment might give rise to riots and disturbances, he consented to go on, and gloomily enough the rest of the journey was accomplished. We had intended returning to Liverpool by the railroad, but Lady W——, who seized upon me in the midst of the crowd, persuaded us to accompany her home, which we gladly did. Lord W—— did not return till past ten o'clock, at which hour he brought the intelligence of Mr Huskisson's death. I need not tell you of the sort of whispering awe which this event threw over our whole circle, and yet, great as was the horror excited by it, I could not help feeling how evanescent the effect of it was after all. The shuddering terror of seeing our fellow-creature thus struck down by our side, and the breathless thankfulness for our own preservation, rendered the first evening of our party at Heaton almost solemn; but the next day the occurrence became a subject of earnest, it is true, but free discussion; and after that, was alluded to with almost as little apparent feeling as if it had not passed under our eyes, and within the space of a few hours.

The Advantages Have Been a Good Deal Overrated

Anonymous ✦ 1830

A traveller recounts his experience of using the railway from both Manchester and Darlington

Manchester to Liverpool line, 1830

LEFT MANCHESTER AT ten o'clock by the railroad for Liverpool. You enter upon it by a staircase through the office from the street at present, but there will, I suppose, be an open entrance bye-and-bye: they have built extensive warehouses adjoining. We were two hours and a half going to Liverpool (about thirty-two miles), and I must think the advantages have been a good deal overrated, for, prejudice apart, I think most people will allow that expedition is the only real advantage gained, the road itself is ugly, though curious and wonderful as a work of art. Near Liverpool it is cut very deeply through rock; and there is a long tunnel which leads into a yard where omnibuses wait to convey passengers to the inns. The tunnel is too low for the engines at present in use, and the carriages are drawn through it by donkeys. The engines are calculated to draw fifty tons. I cannot say that I at all liked it; the speed was too great to be pleasant, and makes you rather giddy, and certainly it is not smoother and easier than a good turnpike road. When the carriages stop or go on, a very violent jolting takes place from the ends of the carriages jostling together. I have heard many say they prefer a horse-coach, but the majority are in favour of the railroad, and they will no doubt knock up the coaches.

Left Manchester by coach at ten o'clock, and arrived in Liverpool by half-past two. The railroad is not supposed to answer vastly well, but they are making a branch to Warrington, which will hurt the Sankey navigation, and throw 1,500 men out of employment: these people are said to be loud in their execrations of it, and to threaten revenge. It is certain the proprietors do not feel easy about it, as one living in Warrington has determined never to go by it, and was coming to Liverpool by coach if there has been room. He would gladly sell his shares. A dividend of 4 per cent has been paid for six months, but money has been borrowed … Charge for tonnage of heavy goods 10s. for thirty-two miles, which appears very dear to me.

Darlington to Stockton line, 11th October 1830
Darlington. Walked to the railroad, which comes within half a mile of the town. Saw a steam-engine drawing about twenty-five waggons, each containing about two tons and a half of coals. A single horse draws four such waggons. I went to Stockton at

four o'clock by coach on the railroad: one horse draws about twenty-four passengers. I did not like it at all, for the road is very ugly in appearance, and being only one line with occasional turns for passing, we were sometimes obliged to wait, and at other times to be drawn back, so that we were full two hours going eleven miles, and they are often more than three hours. There is no other conveyance, as the cheapness has driven the stagecoaches off the road, I only paid 1s. for eleven miles. The motion was very unpleasant – a continual jolting and disagreeable noise.

GREAT WESTERN RAILWAY: AN ETON MASTER OBJECTS

REV. WILLIAM GIFFORD COOKESLEY ✦ 1839

*An Eton Master objects to the proposed
line of the Great Western Railway*

I HAVE BEEN one of the Masters of Eton for about 6 years, I was also an Etonian for about 10 years. I think that the proposed line of railway will be injurious to Eton School, on account of the tone, habit and more especially the wealth and rank of the boys, and it is difficult to avoid the evil, although it might not be so injurious to other schools. The system at Winchester is one of great restraint and coercion compared with ours, our boys are enclosed within certain walls, and taken out to a particular hill for cricket under superintendence. I consider that the prosperity of Eton is mainly owing to the practice of giving the boys as much freedom as possible consistent with discipline, and in the event of a railway passing within a short distance of us, we should be compelled to alter the system, in order to prevent the boys travelling upon it, the principle upon which our prosperity is founded would thus be subverted, which I am sure would be objected to. A railway would afford facilities which the boys would be unable to resist, as they could get out of the reach of school discipline within 30 minutes. I do not think any system of Police could prevent them getting upon it, as the boys do not carry badges upon their backs.

A proposal was made of us not having a Depôt within a certain distance, but we objected to it, also the building of a wall to keep them off: I am satisfied they did not contemplate making it of sufficient length. 2 ½ hours is the longest space of time that can elapse between the absences, and 1 ½ or 1 ¼ hours is the shortest. A boy may be absent 3 times during the day upon a whole holiday, and the head boys in the upper cricket club are allowed to miss a call. If a Clause was inserted stating that no passengers should be taken up or put down within 4 miles, it would not be objectionable.

GREAT WESTERN RAILWAY: A DAIRY FARMER'S VIEW

JOSEPH HULL ✦ 1839

A dairy farmer in the small Wiltshire village of Christian Malford presents his opinions on the Great Western Railway

THE PROPOSED LINE passes through 2½ miles of the Manor of Christian Malford, and cuts across it diagonally, and some part between the canal and the railway will be left very narrow. I rent a Farm of Lord Caernarvon and about half a mile of the richest part of the same will be crossed by the embankment, (the land is not so good at the top of Christian Malford wood as at the bottom) consisting of ploughed, wet, and dairy land, it will separate some of it from the homestead, and divide it in a very inconvenient manner: it will also have the same effect upon Mr Cullamore's farm. My farm consists of nearly 300 acres, 36 or 37 of which are severed by the railway: 2 archways might be sufficient, but it could not then be worked so well as it is at present: I should require more persons to drive the cows, as they would have to go in two different directions. I have 40 cows on my farm, and the archways under the embankment would be injurious to them, and it is necessary to drive them to the homestead and back twice a day. (When large numbers of cows are driven through a small space they injure each other; perhaps 2 or 3 of them would be killed in the course of a month. I should consider 15 feet very narrow for such archways, although accidents do not frequently happen in passing through gates of about 10 feet wide, as the cows go right and left after getting through.) I consider that the extra Haulage to different parts of the farm which the proposed line would cause, and the injury it would be to the cattle, fully equal to £12. or £14. per annum.

The water from these lands drains towards the Avon, and the embankment will have the effect of keeping the water on the lands, as it cuts across the same; but if there are plenty of culverts, and a dyke on each side of the embankment, I think it would improve the drainage.

The proposed line will also be very injurious to the land generally, particularly as it is upon an embankment (some of the fields will be divided into small triangular pieces). I should say that the two other farms upon the estate would not be so good by £20. per annum each and that the value of the manor (which contains 3,000 acres) would be lessened £6,000. There is a very good Turnpike Road through the manor, communicating with Chippenham, which market I attend. The Wilts and Berks Canal passes through my farm, and I can get a hundred tons of manure ... by it in a week, either way: we have a drawbridge over it.

THE COMMUNICATION WITH LONDON IS QUITE SUFFICIENT

EDWARD SHERWOOD ✦ 1839

A farmer in Purley, Berkshire, adds his opinion
to the proposed Great Western Railway

THE PROPOSED LINE passes within ½ a mile of Mr Storer's residence, and would therefore be very prejudicial to his property. I rent the farm which is situated near it, and in the event of the railway being made, I should not expect to pay the same for it. The land required by the railway in this neighbourhood has been valued at £60. per acre, which I do not think sufficient, but if another £60. is added for compensation, it will be quite enough; yet I should not like to dispose of it at that price, taking the inconvenience of severance ... into consideration.

I attend Reading Market, which is a ready money market, one of the best in England; I find the present communications with London quite sufficient; if the more distant towns get equal facilities or communications as Reading, I think that the prosperity of the latter must proportionally diminish. Reading supplies the greater part of the neighbourhood on the Oxfordshire and Berkshire sides of the country, but in the event of the railway being made, some of these places must draw their supplies through it instead of through Reading. I also frequent Newbury market occasionally, but it is not equal to Reading; if there was a railway to Newbury, although Reading would lose, I do not think that Newbury would gain much as there is a Canal to it.

I took some land about 3 months since belonging to Mr Wilder, and some belonging to Mr Powis, which I hold on condition that I shall be remunerated in the event of the railway passing through it, as I consider the land will be injured thereby;

(it would pass through part of it in a tunnel, by which the surface would be preserved). I object to railways generally, as I think they will lessen the agricultural interests, and the importation of Irish cattle, pigs etc. would also be a great detriment to our trade. I do not think I should be benefited even if the proposed line opened an additional market for our produce, as I am satisfied with the present.

INCREASING PROFITS
400 PER CENT

W MEADE WARNER ✦ 1839

*A farmer of Thornly Hall, Oxfordshire, provides evidence
on the proposed London & Birmingham Railway*

I OCCUPY ABOUT 200 acres of land near Leighton Buzzard, and about 400 in Oxfordshire, it is situated about one furlong from the proposed Line. I consider it to be an essential service to myself and the farmers on the line; had it passed 10 or 15 years ago it would have been a benefit to me of not less than £50. per annum. The farming of grass land in particular would be considerably improved; we should be able to send to London much better kind of produce. Lambs are sent to London from our neighbourhood by waggons, which occupies a space of 24 hours; but they are usually sent on the road, which prevents us sending many, as they have not the strength to bear the journey; if a railroad was established no doubt the farmers would send more; it is important to send them early in the season, as they would feed off sooner. At Hemel Hempstead, and down in Buckinghamshire, below us, they send calves, to which the same observations will apply. I have been a Dairyman 20 years and have 40 or 50 cows, and I consider that a railway would be still more important to the dairy farmers, as they would be able to send milk and butter to the London Market. I had offers made to me to supply a part of London with milk, but I could not undertake it for want of a conveyance; if we could get a railroad we should increase the profits 400 or 500 per cent on milk and butter…

In the heavy seasons 1,500 head of cattle pass through Hockcliffe to London weekly on the line of road parallel to the proposed Railway … they are considerably injured by being driven up, it would be a great advantage to send them by a railroad, even if it was dearer; sometimes the poor things are driven until their feet become sore, they are consequently sold on the road for what they will fetch, they are often driven until they have not a foot to stand on; if I paid double for transmitting my cattle I should be a very great gainer; besides the cruelty and exposure, they are a very great nuisance on the public roads, to carriages, etc. There are not less than 10,000 head of sheep pass weekly. They are driven 40 miles at about 1s. per head. I should not imagine sheep sent by the railroad would be liable to be heated or hurt by rubbing against each other. There is a considerable quantity of poultry reared about us, much of it goes to Aylesbury. A rapid communication with the London market would be an advantage to both the suppliers and consumers of poultry. Our lands are principally heavy, but potatoes might be grown and sent up, and at other parts of the line garden produce might be cultivated. The manufacture of straw plait is carried on very largely in our neighbourhood; it is sent principally to Dunstable and the vicinity, some of it is manufactured into hats and bonnets at Liverpool, and some at Luton. I conceive a railroad would be advantageous to the buyers. I am a proprietor as well as an occupier, my property lies in land; I believe my estates along the line would be increased in value 30 per cent.

A GREAT CONVENIENCE
TO MANUFACTURERS

OLIVER MASON ✦ 1839

A merchant speaks in favour of the proposed
London & Birmingham route

I WAS A MERCHANT and an inhabitant of Birmingham
23 years. I was also High Bailiff for that town last year ... The
opening of canals was a great benefit to the town, and an
increased communication would be a greater advantage to them,
particularly as merchants. We are often put to great loss, and
cannot execute orders for want of time, if we lose the opportunity
of shipping by a certain vessel which only sails once a year from
a port we lose the order; our correspondent says, 'If you can ship
my goods by such a ship send them, and if you cannot, do not
send them.' A railway would also be a great convenience to
manufacturers, they would be able to calculate to a day the
delivery of their goods and be enabled to compete more
successfully with the great opposition they experienced from
Foreign Merchants; at Altona and Liege they have made such
extraordinary progress during the last few years, that we are
beaten out of the Italian, Spanish, and Portuguese Markets, as
they can get the raw materials cheaper than we can; we excel
them in dispatch and expedition of orders. They are establishing
a railway from the Hague to Antwerp; they frequently undersell
us, and we require every possible advantage to enable us to meet
the foreign manufacturers. In manufacturing towns the
population do not work the first days in the week, it is only
at the latter end that the great strain of business is brought into
the market. ...

The railway likewise offers an advantage in reference to St
Petersburgh. I had an order for St Petersburgh, and the goods

arrived so late that the last vessel was on the point of sailing, we might have got them if we had only two days more. The line of communication with the West Indies and America from Birmingham is principally through Liverpool, although there is much through London. Canal communication is inconvenient from the stoppages; I once had an action brought against me for the freight of some goods which I engaged to ship, they were detained by a stoppage of the canal, and I was called on to pay the freight although the goods were returned upon my hands.

I HATE
RAILROADS!

ANONYMOUS ✦ 1839

*A traveller shares a multitude of complaints
about a railway trip to Manchester*

I HATE RAILROADS. Any one can love railroads, or like railroads, or praise railroads – but I hate railroads. I hate to be obliged to arrive at a railroad office a quarter of an hour before starting. I hate to be obliged to go and stand between certain pieces of wood nailed across and along to ask for a place. I hate to be made to go in at one end, and out at the other just as if I had already commenced my imprisonment, and as though the turnkey had fastened down upon me all his iron, steam and coals. I hate to see all my luggage and baggage taken from me, and placed, *malgré moi* on a stone pavement, quite naked and unprotected – boxes, trunks, shawls, ruffs, books, umbrellas, maps, sandwich boxes, all in one *hurly-burly* – and then to be told that I may go and claim my luggage, and arrange my luggage, just as I like. I hate to have to do with porters who never touch their hats, and who cannot be civil, because you are forbidden to

give them a silver sixpence. I believe the poor fellows have not
even pockets in their breeches, lest a stray shilling should by
chance find its way into them. I hate to be made to wait for a
steam-engine, and for a steam-engine never to wait for me.
Horses will wait, and men will wait – and even sometimes, when
you are young and handsome, or old and wealthy – or neither,
and very agreeable (precisely my case) women or ladies will wait
for you (ay, and the Lancashire witches too); but a steam-engine
will not wait, for all its enjoyment appears to consist in rattling
away as hard as its lungs will admit, from Dan to Beersheba, and
from London to Jericho, without so much as kissing its hand to
the nymphs and maidens on the road. Then I hate to be
'numbered'. I had rather be named than numbered – and both
are very disagreeable. To think that I was No. 71, and my
daughter No. 73, though I am only 40, and my daughter only
18. It is a monstrously unpleasant thing when the 'guard' asks
No. 71 if he will give his ticket, and if No. 74 wishes to get out at
'Tring'. Then sometimes No. 74 'takes the liberty of observing to
No. 70 that it is a very fine day' – and 'begs pardon of No. 72,
and would be glad to know if he would have any objection to
change places?' This ticketing system looks so much like the
incipient portion of prison discipline—like the preparatory steps
of a police surveillance...

Then I hate to be boxed in the rail coach or rail waggon, with
a projecting impediment against all love and affection between
myself and my next-door neighbour. Why, some of the
pleasantest hours of my life have been, when some soft, gentle
creature, in the form of a female stage-coach companion,
overcome by sleep, or wearied out with laughing, has at last
placed her soft head on my soft shoulder, and gently slept for
some two hours, unconscious of all that was passing around her,
and absorbed in visions of bliss, or in dreams of nothingness.
But none of these shoulderings, none of these tender and delicate

attentions can be practised or enjoyed in a steam carriage. Oh, no! on the monster goes, sometimes at 20, then at 30, and often at 40 miles per hour, hissing, foaming, firing, snorting, groaning, and even bellowing, dragging behind so many isolated beings, all divided by bits of lined and padded wood, called 'head cushions', from each other, unable to speak to a neighbour, much less to make love to one. The man who invented such contrivances as these was some fierce Malthusian, some unregenerated Godwin, some deplorable, cross, fusty, wretched disappointed, ugly old bachelor, who, after having made as many offers of marriage as he was years old, took to hating the softer sex, and condemning the rest of his species to travel with some No. 75 or 77, in a coach from London to Manchester, without scarcely being able even to see her features.

Then I hate to be fastened in a coach from which I cannot escape, except with the *certainty* of immediate death, without the permission of a steam-engine. I have seen horses for forty years. I have seen them on a theatre and on a field of battle; in a camp, stable, a carriage, a palace, a drawing-room; and everywhere I have found them obedient, tractable, kind-hearted, gentle, timid, noble. When I say 'whoh,' or 'whoa,' to a horse, why, he whohs at once – or, in plain English, he stops. But you may say or shout, 'whoh,' or 'whoa,' to a steam-engine, till your very heart burst, and he will pay no attention to you whatever. There you are, six of you, isolated, each so many inches of coach, great or small, Daniel Lambert or good Mr Beardsall, the anti-intemperance Baptist minister of Manchester, as thin as a shaving, and quite as dry – you must all have the same number of inches and no intrusion on the territory of your neighbour. Yes, there you are, fastened in, boxed in, so well secured, that if you had to make O'Rourke's journey to the moon and back again [from a story by Thomas Crofton Croker], you need not be afraid of being jolted out. How infinitely preferable is the dear, old-fashioned system! When there is a long hill and a fine prospect, the horses stop, the guard gets down, opens the door, invites you to alight – you offer your arm to a lady – or, what is still, more agreeable, the rest of your fellow-travellers descend, but the lady 'prefers your pleasant society', and remains *tete-a-tete* with you, whilst thoughts breathe and words burn. But nothing of this '*sentimental*' travelling ever takes place in a railway coach. Poor Sterne would have been sadly put to it, if he had thus been compelled to journey in the French provinces! Then I hate never to be jolted, never to be rumbled about, to be whirled along iron bars, just like bales of goods, without a road, and only with rails.

Then I hate not to alight when the horses ought to change; and when coals are taken in, instead of a fresh team, and cold water, instead of oats and beans. I hate not to hear the horses shake themselves, after having run their stage, not to see fresh and bright blood four-in-hand, harnessed so brightly and looking so pretty and prancing; readying for starting, waiting our arrival; not to receive the visit of the agile bar-maid, or buxom landlady, arranging their lips so invitingly, and asking you, 'if you would like to take something?' Why are we to be deprived of their soft and sweet invitation, only to have in exchange the groanings of a huge iron tea-kettle, bursting with rage, or with steam? I do protest most heartily against this substitution of ugliness for beauty, hot steam for sweet breath, and angry roaring for smiling looks.

Then I hate it 'to be expected' that I am to eat Banbury cakes, and drink bottled ale at a precise distance from London, and so to eat and so to drink, wet or dry, light or dark, cold or warm, in the open air. No soup – no glass of hot brandy and water – no ham sandwich – no quiet mutton chop just done to a turn, and all ready for eating in a quarter of an hour – no dinner – no breakfast – no, Banbury cakes and cold ale, from January to July, and from July to January. 'If this monopoly shall be submitted to,' said I, 'we shall soon be prohibited from eating and drinking anything else; and besides this, we shall be compelled each man to eat so many cakes and drink so much beer.'

Then I hate to go every where at the same rate. Over the moor – through (not up) the hill – along the valley – across the river – every where, though, the country be dull and uninteresting, verdant and laughing, or bold and romantic – every where, along we rattle and along we roar at the rate of forty miles per hour, excluding stoppages. I once saw an Englishman (but then he had a cork leg) stump through the Louvre in sixteen minutes. He boasted of his *feats* of rapidity, though he had but one foot, and I believe he undertook to see Europe in a month. Just so acts that steam-engine fellow, who drags you along up hill and down dale, without giving you permission or time even to exclaim, 'How beautiful!'

Then I hate the horrible shriek of the wheels and carriages some three minutes before they stop, so horrible that your very teeth chatter, and your very head and ears ache or burn. I hope Dr Lardner [an 18th-century theologian] will have the politeness to examine this *crying* evil, and invent some remedy for this awful system of setting our 'teeth on edge'. Should he not succeed in this matter, iron railways will soon be deserted.

Then I hate not to be allowed a moment's time to tell a fellow-traveller, ' Do look at Stafford Castle,' for before I have finished my sentence, we are a mile off. And I hate not to have a minute even to look at the Cheshire hills … but to be hurried by them all as if it were a sin to look at a hill, and an offence against nature to admire a mountain.

Then I hate the insolent notice to passengers, couched in the following terms, as though the steam directors were government inspectors of their passengers' health and stomachs:

'No smoking is allowed in the station houses.
A substantial (hang their impudence!) breakfast
may be had at the station house at Birmingham,
by parties going by the early train; but no person
is allowed to sell liquors or eatables of any kind
upon the line.'

Now, really this way of treating 'their patrons the public' I do
hate most cordially. Why should not *late* breakfasts be allowed, as
well as early ones? And why should not 'light' breakfasts be
allowed, as well as substantial ones? And why should not smoking
be allowed in the station houses? Surely we do not travel by
gunpowder, as well as by steam. If we did, there might be some
danger in a cigar, but there can be none possibly from smoking
in a station house...

Then I hate to be left alone without the engine at all, as I was
lately between Wolverhampton and Stafford, because the engine
would not work well, and on it ran alone, leaving all the carriages
forsaken, whilst the engine, being first unyoked, worked its course
to Pankridge, and there got mended. Some three quarters of an
hour afterwards the passengers heard it roaring back again; and
then again we were dragged, nothing loath, the rest of our way.
The guard gave no explanation. Horses there were none;
coachmen none. The engineer had bratted off with the engine.
And the '*boxed-up*', *well-imprisoned* passengers, were obliged to
remain in quietness and sulkiness, till it pleased the master
to return. Then I hate to have a leg torn off my poor body if I
get out of a carriage before it is locked, or an arm quietly born
away in triumph by another train, if I happen to put it for a
moment out of the window; or both eyes put out with dust and
scalding steam, if I only forgot to close the windows as we pass
through a tunnel. Then I hate not to be able to stop in less than
five minutes, and then at some three miles distant, in case I desire

to change my route, or alight, or should illness suddenly assail either myself or a fellow-passenger. Then I hate, when I arrive at the end of the journey, to have to watch for my luggage as a cat does for a mouse, and pounce upon it and drag it away (in spite of the furies) or else have it carried off in triumph by some one more nimble than myself. Then I hate to have to travel some two miles from the station house to the town or city to which I am about to proceed, though the night be dark and gloomy, and though the train be some hours 'en retard'. All this I hate – yes, hate most cordially; and so, really and truly, I hate railroads!

THE LAKE DISTRICT: LET THE BEAUTY BE UNDISFIGURED

WILLIAM WORDSWORTH • 1844

In a letter to the Morning Post, *the poet gives his objections to the Kendal and Windermere Railway*

Sonnet on the Projected Kendal and Windermere Railway

> Is then no nook of English ground secure
> From rash assault? Schemes of retirement sown
> In youth, and mid the busy world kept pure
> As when their earliest flowers of hope were blown,
> Must perish; – how can they this blight endure?
> And must he too the ruthless change bemoan
> Who scorns a false utilitarian lure
> Mid his paternal fields at random thrown?
> Baffle the threat, bright Scene, from Orrest-head
> Given to the pausing traveller's rapturous glance:
> Plead for thy peace, thou beautiful romance

Of nature; and, if human hearts be dead,
Speak, passing winds; ye torrents, with your strong
And constant voice, protest against the wrong.

Rydal Mount, 16th October 1844

TO THE EDITOR of the *Morning Post*

SIR, Some little time ago you did me the favour of inserting a sonnet expressive of the regret and indignation which, in common with others all over these Islands, I felt at the proposal of a railway to extend from Kendal to Low Wood, near the head of Windermere. The project was so offensive to a large majority of the proprietors through whose lands the line, after it came in view of the Lake, was to pass, that, for this reason, and the avowed one of the heavy expense without which the difficulties in the way could not be overcome, it has been partially abandoned, and the terminus is now announced to be at a spot within a mile of Bowness. But as no guarantee can be given that the project will not hereafter be revived, and an attempt made to carry the line forward through the vales of Ambleside and Grasmere, and as in one main particular the case remains essentially the same, allow me to address you upon certain points which merit more consideration than the favourers of the scheme have yet given them. The matter, though seemingly local, is really one in which all persons of taste must be interested…

I shall barely touch upon the statistics of the question, leaving these to the two adverse parties, who will lay their several statements before the Board of Trade, which may possibly be induced to refer the matter to the House of Commons; and, contemplating that possibility, I hope that the observations I have to make may not be altogether without influence upon the public, and upon individuals whose duty it may be to decide in their place whether the proposed measure shall be referred to a Committee of the House. Were the case before us an ordinary one, I should reject such an attempt as presumptuous and futile; but it is not only different from all others, but, in truth, peculiar.

In this district the manufactures are trifling; mines it has none, and its quarries are either wrought out or superseded; the soil is light, and the cultivateable parts of the country are very limited; so that it has little to send out, and little has it also to receive. Summer TOURISTS, (and the very word precludes the notion of a railway) it has in abundance; but the inhabitants are so few and their intercourse with other places so infrequent, that one daily coach, which could not be kept going but through its connection with the Post-office, suffices for three-fourths of the year along the line of country as far as Keswick. The staple of the district is, in fact, its beauty and its character of seclusion and retirement; and to these topics and to others connected with them my remarks shall be confined.

The projectors have induced many to favour their schemes by declaring that one of their main objects is to place the beauties of the Lake District within easier reach of those who cannot afford to pay for ordinary conveyances. Look at the facts. Railways are completed, which, joined with others in rapid progress, will bring travellers who prefer approaching by Ullswater to within four miles of that lake. The Lancaster and Carlisle Railway will approach the town of Kendal, about eight or nine miles from eminences that command the whole vale of Windermere. The Lakes are therefore at present of very easy access for all persons; but if they be not made still more so, the poor, it is said, will be wronged. Before this be admitted let the question be fairly looked into, and its different bearings examined. No one can assert that, if this … approach be not effected, anything will be taken away that is actually possessed. …

Why, to show that a vivid perception of romantic scenery is neither inherent in mankind, nor a necessary consequence of even a comprehensive education. It is benignly ordained that green fields, clear blue skies, running streams of pure water, rich groves and woods, orchards, and all the ordinary varieties of rural Nature, should find an easy way to the affections of all men, and more or less so from early childhood till the senses are impaired by old age and the sources of mere earthly enjoyment have in a great measure failed. But a taste beyond this, however desirable it may be that every one should possess it, is not to be implanted at once; it must be gradually developed both in nations and individuals. Rocks and mountains, torrents and wide-spread waters, and all those features of Nature which go to the composition of such scenes as this part of England is distinguished for, cannot, in their finer relations to the human mind, be comprehended, or even very imperfectly conceived, without processes of culture or opportunities of observation in some degree habitual. In the eye of thousands and tens of thousands, a rich meadow, with fat cattle grazing upon it, or the sight of what they would call a heavy crop of corn, is worth all that the Alps and Pyrenees in their utmost grandeur and beauty could show to them; and, notwithstanding the grateful influence, as we have observed, of ordinary Nature and the productions of the fields, it is noticeable what trifling conventional prepossessions will, in common minds, not only preclude pleasure from the sight of natural beauty, but will even turn it into an object of disgust. 'If I had to do with this garden,' said a respectable person, one of my neighbours, 'I would sweep away all the black and dirty stuff from that wall.' The wall was backed by a bank of earth, and was exquisitely decorated with ivy, flowers, moss, and ferns, such as grow of themselves in like places; but the mere notion of fitness associated with a trim garden-wall prevented, in this instance, all sense of the spontaneous bounty and delicate care of Nature. In the midst of a small pleasure-ground, immediately below my house, rises a detached rock, equally remarkable for the beauty of its form, the ancient oaks that grow out of it, and the flowers and shrubs which adorn it. 'What a nice place would this be,' said a Manchester tradesman, pointing to the rock, 'if that ugly lump were but out of the way.' Men as little advanced in the pleasure which such objects give to others are so far from being rare, that they may be said fairly to represent a large majority of mankind. This is a fact, and none but the deceiver and the willingly deceived can be offended by its being stated. But as a more susceptible taste is undoubtedly a great acquisition, and has been spreading among us for some years, the question is, what means are most likely to be beneficial in extending its operation? Surely that good is not to be obtained by transferring at once uneducated persons in large bodies to particular spots, where the combinations of natural objects are such as would afford the greatest pleasure to those who have been in the habit of observing and studying the peculiar character of such scenes, and how they differ one from another. Instead of tempting artisans and labourers, and the humbler classes of shopkeepers, to ramble to a distance, let us rather look with lively sympathy upon persons in that condition, when, upon a holiday, or on the Sunday, after having attended divine worship, they make little excursions with their wives and children among neighbouring fields, whither the whole of each family might stroll, or be conveyed at much less cost than would be required to take a single individual of the number to the shores of Windermere by the cheapest conveyance. It is in some such way as this only, that persons who must labour daily with their hands for bread in large towns, or are subject to confinement through the week, can be trained to a profitable intercourse with Nature where she is the most distinguished by the majesty and sublimity of her forms. ...

And wherever any one among the labouring classes has made even an approach to the sensibility which drew a lamentation from Burns when he had uprooted a daisy with his plough, and caused him to turn the 'weeder-clips aside' from the thistle, and spare 'the symbol dear' of his country, then surely such a one, could he afford by any means to travel as far as Kendal, would not grudge a two hours' walk across the skirts of the beautiful country that he was desirous of visiting.

The wide-spread waters of these regions are in their nature peaceful; so are the steep mountains and the rocky glens; nor can they be profitably enjoyed but by a mind disposed to peace. Go to a pantomime, a farce, or a puppet-show, if you want noisy pleasure – the crowd of spectators who partake your enjoyment will, by their presence and acclamations, enhance it; but may those who have given proof that they prefer other gratifications continue to be safe from the molestation of cheap trains pouring out their hundreds at a time along the margin of Windermere; nor let any one be liable to the charge of being selfishly disregardful of the poor, and their innocent and salutary enjoyments, if he does not congratulate himself upon the especial benefit which would thus be conferred on such a concourse. …

What can, in truth, be more absurd, than that either rich or poor should be spared the trouble of travelling by the high roads over so short a space, according to their respective means, if the unavoidable consequence must be a great disturbance of the retirement, and in many places a destruction of the beauty of the country, which the parties are come in search of? Would not this be pretty much like the child's cutting up his drum to learn where the sound came from?

Having, I trust, given sufficient reason for the belief that the imperfectly educated classes are not likely to draw much good from rare visits to the Lakes performed in this way, and surely on their own account it is not desirable that the visits should be frequent, let us glance at the mischief which such facilities would certainly produce. The directors of railway companies are always ready to devise or encourage entertainments for tempting the humbler classes to leave their homes. Accordingly, for the profit of the shareholders and that of the lower class of innkeepers, we should have wrestling matches, horse and boat races without number, and pot-houses and beer-shops would keep pace with these excitements and recreations, most of which might too easily be had elsewhere. The injury which would thus be done to morals, both among this influx of strangers and the lower class of inhabitants, is obvious; and, supposing such extraordinary temptations not to be held out, there cannot be a doubt that the Sabbath day in the towns of Bowness and Ambleside, and other parts of the district, would be subject to much additional desecration.

Whatever comes of the scheme which we have endeavoured to discountenance, the charge against its opponents of being selfishly regardless of the poor, ought to cease. The cry has been raised and kept up by three classes of persons – they who wish to bring into discredit all such as stand in the way of their gains or gambling speculations; they who are dazzled by the application of physical science to the useful arts, and indiscriminately applaud what they call the spirit of the age as manifested in this way; and, lastly, those persons who are ever ready to step forward in what appears to them to be the cause of the poor, but not always with becoming attention to particulars. I am well aware that upon the first class what has been said will be of no avail, but upon the two latter some impression will, I trust, be made.

To conclude. The railway power, we know well, will not admit of being materially counteracted by sentiment; and who would wish it where large towns are connected, and the interests of trade and agriculture are substantially promoted, by such mode of intercommunication? But be it remembered, that this case is, as has been said before, a peculiar one, and that the staple of the country is its beauty and its character of retirement. Let then the beauty be undisfigured and the retirement unviolated, unless there be reason for believing that rights and interests of a higher kind and more apparent than those which have been urged in behalf of the projected intrusion will compensate the sacrifice. Thanking you for the judicious observations that have appeared in your paper upon the subject of railways,

I remain, Sir,
Your obliged,
WM WORDSWORTH

WE HAVE TOO MUCH HURRYING ABOUT IN THESE ISLANDS

WILLIAM WORDSWORTH ✦ 1844

In a second letter to the Morning Post, *the poet further explains his views*

Rydal Mount, 9th December 1844

TO THE EDITOR of the *Morning Post*

Sir, As you obligingly found space in your journal for observations of mine upon the intended Kendal and Windermere Railway, I venture to send you some further remarks upon the same subject. The scope of the main argument, it will be recollected, was to prove that the perception of what has acquired the name of picturesque and romantic scenery is so far from being intuitive, that it can be produced only by a slow and gradual process of culture; and to show, as a consequence, that the humbler ranks of society are not, and cannot be, in a state to gain material benefit from a more speedy access than they now have to this beautiful region. Some of our opponents dissent from this latter proposition, though the most judicious of them readily admit the former; but then, overlooking not only positive assertions, but reasons carefully given, they say, 'As you allow that a more comprehensive taste is desirable, you ought to side with us'; and they illustrate their position, by reference to the British Museum and National Picture Gallery. 'There,' they add, 'thanks to the easy entrance now granted, numbers are seen, indicating by their dress and appearance their humble condition, who, when admitted for the first time, stare vacantly around them, so that one is inclined to ask what brought them hither? But an impression is made, something gained which may induce them to repeat the visit until light breaks in upon them, and they take an intelligent interest in what they behold.' Persons who talk thus forget that, to produce such an improvement, frequent access at small cost of time and labour is indispensable. Manchester lies, perhaps, within eight hours' railway distance of London; but surely no one would advise that Manchester operatives should contract a habit of running to and fro between that town and London, for the sake of forming an intimacy with the British Museum and National Gallery? No, no; little would all but a very few gain from the opportunities which, consistently with common sense, could be afforded them for such expeditions. Nor would it fare better with them in respect of trips to the Lake District; an assertion, the truth of which no one can doubt, who has learned by experience how many men of the same or higher rank, living from their birth in this very region, are indifferent to those objects around them in which a cultivated taste takes so much pleasure. I should not have detained the reader so long upon this point, had I not heard (glad tidings for the directors and traffickers in shares!) that among the affluent and benevolent manufacturers of Yorkshire and Lancashire are some who already entertain the thought of sending, at their own expense, large bodies of their workmen, by railway, to the banks of Windermere. Surely those gentlemen will think a little more before they put such a scheme into practice. The rich man cannot benefit the poor, nor the superior the inferior, by anything that degrades him. Packing off men after this fashion, for holiday entertainment, is, in fact, treating them like children. They go at the will of their master, and must return at the same, or they will be dealt with as transgressors. ...

Consider also the state of the Lake District; and look, in the first place, at the little town of Bowness, in the event of such railway inundations. What would become of it in this, not the Retreat, but the Advance, of the Ten Thousand? Leeds, I am told, has sent as many at once to Scarborough. We should have the whole of Lancashire, and no small part of Yorkshire, pouring in upon us to meet the men of Durham, and the borderers from Cumberland and Northumberland. Alas, alas, if the lakes are to pay this penalty for their own attractions! ...

But with the fear before me of the line being carried; at a day not distant, through the whole breadth of the district, I could dwell, with much concern for other residents, upon the condition which they would be in if that outrage should be committed; nor ought it to be deemed impertinent were I to recommend this point to the especial regard of Members of Parliament who may have to decide upon the question. The two Houses of Legislature have frequently shown themselves not unmindful of private feeling in these matters. They have, in some cases, been induced to spare parks and pleasure grounds. But along the great railway lines these are of rare occurrence. They are but a part, and a small part; here it is far otherwise. Among the ancient inheritances of the yeomen, surely worthy of high respect, are interspersed through the entire district villas, most of them with such small domains attached that the occupants would be hardly less annoyed by a railway passing through their neighbour's ground than through their own. And it would be unpardonable not to advert to the effect of this measure on the interests of the very poor in this locality. With the town of Bowness I have no minute acquaintance; but of Ambleside, Grasmere, and the neighbourhood, I can testify from long experience, that they have been favoured by the residence of a gentry whose love of retirement has been a blessing to these vales; for their families have ministered, and still minister, to the temporal and spiritual necessities of the poor, and have personally superintended the education of the children in a degree which does those benefactors the highest honour, and which is, I trust, gratefully acknowledged in the hearts of all whom they have relieved, employed, and taught. Many of those friends of our poor would quit this country if the apprehended change were realised, and would be succeeded by strangers not linked to the neighbourhood, but flitting to and fro between their fancy villas and the homes where their wealth was accumulated and accumulating by trade and manufactures. It is obvious that persons, so unsettled, whatever might be their good wishes and readiness to part with money for charitable purposes, would ill supply the loss of the inhabitants who had been driven away.

It will be felt by those who think with me upon this occasion that I have been writing on behalf of a social condition which no one who is competent to judge of it will be willing to subvert, and that I have been endeavouring to support moral sentiments and intellectual pleasures of a high order against an enmity which seems growing more and more formidable every day; I mean 'Utilitarianism', serving as a mask for cupidity and gambling speculations. My business with this evil lies in its reckless mode of action by Railways, now its favourite instruments. Upon good authority I have been told that there was lately an intention of driving one of these pests, as they are likely too often to prove, through a part of the magnificent ruins of Furness Abbey -- an outrage which was prevented by some one pointing out how easily a deviation might be made; and the hint produced its due effect upon the engineer. ...

Similar remarks might be applied to the mountainous country of Wales; but there too, the plea of utility, especially as expediting the communication between England and Ireland, more than justifies the labours of the Engineer. Not so would it be with the Lake District. A railroad is already planned along the sea coast, and another from Lancaster to Carlisle is in great forwardness: an intermediate one is therefore, to say the least of it, superfluous. Once and for all let me declare that it is not against Railways but against the abuse of them that I am contending. ...

I have now done with the subject. The time of life at which I have arrived may, I trust, if nothing else will, guard me from the imputation of having written from any selfish interests, or from fear of disturbance which a railway might cause to myself. If gratitude for what repose and quiet in a district hitherto, for the most part, not disfigured but beautified by human hands, have done for me through the course of a long life, and hope that others might hereafter be benefited in the same manner and in the same country, be selfishness, then, indeed, but not otherwise, I plead guilty to the charge. Nor have I opposed this undertaking on account of the inhabitants of the district merely, but, as hath been intimated, for the sake of every one, however humble his condition, who coming hither shall bring with him an eye to perceive, and a heart to feel and worthily enjoy. And as for holiday pastimes, if a scene is to be chosen suitable ... for persons thronging from a distance, it may be found elsewhere at less cost of every kind. But, in fact, we have too much hurrying about in these islands; much for idle pleasure, and more from over activity in the pursuit of wealth, without regard to the good or happiness of others.

Proud were ye, Mountains, when, in times of old,
Your patriot sons, to stem invasive war,
Intrenched your brows; ye gloried in each scar:
Now, for your shame, a Power, the Thirst of Gold,
That rules o'er Britain like a baneful star,
Wills that your peace, your beauty, shall be sold,
And clear way made for her triumphal car
Through the beloved retreats your arms enfold!
Heard YE that Whistle? As her long-linked Train
Swept onwards, did the vision cross your view?
Yes, ye were startled; – and, in balance true,
Weighing the mischief with the promised gain,
Mountains, and Vales, and Floods, I call on you
To share the passion of a just disdain.

WM WORDSWORTH

A Visit to the Crystal Palace

Charlotte Brontë ✦ 1851

*In a letter to her father, the author mentions
her impressions of the Great Exhibition*

YESTERDAY I WENT for the second time to the Crystal Palace. We remained in it about three hours, and I must say I was more struck with it on this occasion than at my first visit. It is a wonderful place – vast, strange, new, and impossible to describe. Its grandeur does not consist in *one* thing, but in the unique assemblage of *all* things. Whatever human industry has created, you find there, from the great compartments filled with railway engines and boilers, with mill-machinery in

full work, with splendid carriages of all kinds, with harness of
every description – to the glass-covered and velvet-spread stands
loaded with the most gorgeous work of the goldsmith and
silversmith, and the carefully guarded caskets full of real
diamonds and pearls worth hundreds of thousands of pounds.
It may be called a bazaar or a fair, but it is such a bazaar or fair
as Eastern genii might have created. It seems as if magic only
could have gathered this mass of wealth from all the ends of the
earth – as if none but supernatural hands could have arranged it
thus, with such a blaze and contrast of colours and marvellous
power of effect. The multitude filling the great aisles seems ruled
and subdued by some invisible influence. Amongst the thirty
thousand souls that peopled it the day I was there, not one loud
noise was to be heard, not one irregular movement seen – the
living tide rolls on quietly, with a deep hum like the sea heard
from the distance.

Getting to the
Great Exhibition

M Saul ✦ 1851

A letter to the Preston Chronicle *relates the difficulties
regional visitors to the Exhibition faced*

To the Editor of the *Preston Chronicle*

Sir, It is now definitely fixed upon that on the 21st,
and following Saturdays, persons will be conveyed by railway
from Preston to London and back for £1 3s., allowing a period
of seven or fourteen days in London. At this particular season,
I fear, few of the working classes can spare time and money for
such a journey. However, setting that part of the matter aside,
I think the time of the train's arrival in the metropolis is a most

unfavourable one to strangers; for they reach their destination about twelve o'clock on Saturday night, a most unseasonable hour for those who are unacquainted with London, and more especially if they have not made previous arrangements with regard to lodgings, etc. It appears strange why the Lancaster & Carlisle Company should have fixed upon Saturday afternoons as the time of departure from Preston. Why not have fixed upon some particular day earlier in the week, by the evening express train? By this course, excursionists would reach London at an early hour in the morning, and much difficulty would be avoided. It would have been much better, too, I think, if parties would have been allowed to return at *any time* during the fourteen days they are permitted to stay in London. Those not overstocked with money would be enabled to return home if they thought proper in one or two days, as the case might be, and avoid the great outlay which necessarily attends a visit to the metropolis, by providing food previous to leaving home.

By allowing these remarks a place in the *Chronicle*, it may perhaps be the means of the day of departure from Preston, by the low fare, being altered, so as to suit better the parties for whose benefit the reduced fare is intended.

I am, Sir, yours very truly,
M SAUL
Garstang, 18th June 1851

RAILWAY FARES TO
THE EXHIBITION

A WORKING MAN ✦ 1851

A York resident is exercised by the
rail fares to and from the Great Exhibition

TO THE EDITOR of the *York Herald*

Sir, There are few towns in this county where a stronger
desire has been shewn by the higher and middle classes, to assist
the working man to witness the Great Exhibition, than the city
of York. Clubs have been formed in every town and village, to
give an opportunity for the working man to accumulate means
by his own exertions, but a number of our citizens have so
generously come forward to assist the working men of this city,
that few would have the excuse of being unable to attend...

The fare from York to London, 3rd class, is 18s. The fare
from Hull to London is, 3rd class: 10s., 17s. 2nd class and 23s. 1st
class. The 23s. 1st class having the privilege of returning by any
train (the express excepted), at once making a difference of 8s.
on each passenger travelling by the 3rd class, and tantamount to
taxing the latter amount from the generous subscriptions of our
citizens. The high price of fares alone has been the strongest
motive for so large a number withdrawing their deposits from
the working men's club. Unequal fares for the working classes
does not appear to be confined to the railway alone, as the Ariel
steam-boat comes from Hull next Monday – fares, best cabin, 1s.
6d., fore cabin, 1s. – the same boat ... advertised to go back from
York the following Thursday to Hull and back, fore cabin, 2s.,
best cabin, 3s. Why York should be so favoured, appears a query.

Yours respectfully,
A WORKING MAN
St. Sampson's, York, 26th June 1851

GROWTH AND EXPLORATION

1851–1900

The second half of the 19th century saw Britain's railway network continue to expand. While there had once been a plethora of small local railway companies, a pattern of amalgamations and takeovers led to the growth of mighty, and highly profitable, railway empires, each controlling thousands of miles of lines. Important trunk routes that we know today, such as the East Coast and West Coast main lines, were born in the early years of this period.

Within a short time the rapid development of steam locomotive design, coupled with the introduction of steel rails and safety features such as block signalling and vacuum brakes, all contributed to a faster and safer railway system. Railway works and towns, such as Swindon and Crewe, sprouted up from green-field sites, with the workers and their families looked after from the cradle to the grave by their paternalistic employers. Railway architecture reached new heights of grandeur, culminating in William Barlow's St Pancras station, which opened as the London terminus of the Midland Railway in 1868.

Railway civil engineering also reached new heights during this period – the Midland Railway's Settle & Carlisle line, which was built by an army of 6,000 'navvies' at enormous expense across and through the rugged Pennines, was the pinnacle of Victorian engineering when it opened in 1876. John Fowler and Benjamin Baker's iconic Forth Bridge was an engineering marvel when it opened in 1890 – and still is today.

'MY HEART'S IN THE HIGHLANDS'

ANDREW HALLIDAY ✦ 1865

A Scots sketchwriter and protégé of Charles Dickens shares
his experiences of travelling in the Scottish Highlands

I LEAVE BANFF, and make my way westward by such a queer little railway! An innocent railway I should call it; a railway that wouldn't kill a fly, much less a human passenger. I believe there never was but one accident on this railway, and that was on the opening-day, when the engine, not being used to it, ran off the rails, and tumbled all the directors into the ditch. The legend goes that the directors picked themselves up, adjourned to a neighbouring and hospitable farm-house, and celebrated the auspicious occasion over several tumblers of toddy, while their anxious relatives were searching in vain among the wreck of the carriages for any trace of their mangled remains.

I am the only passenger this morning at the Banff station. Solely on my account a square box upon wheels, drawn by two horses, and known here as '*the* omnibus', has rattled up from the Fife Arms Hotel; solely on my account is the ticket-office opened; and for me and me alone do fire burn and water boil, and guard and stoker and engine-driver attend to perform their various duties. Seated in my carriage, waiting for the train to start, I overhear something like the following conversation, the interlocutors being the guard and the engine-driver: 'Ony body else comin'?' 'I dinna see ony body.' 'Weel, time's up, we maun start.' 'Stop a minute.' 'Didna ye say the druggist was ga'in' wi' us this morning?' (This to the clerk, who responds in the affirmative.) 'Weel, jist rin out and see if he's coming.' 'Stop a minute, Geordie, here's somebody.' Somebody walks in and takes his seat quite leisurely. 'Ony mair coming?' 'Na, nae mair that I can see.' 'Oh, weel, we winna wite ony langer.' And the train, with two passengers in it (there would have been only one if time had been kept), moves slowly out of the station. This northern railway has many simple and innocent ways. It has only a single line of rails; the engine-driver and guard are on the most intimate terms with the passengers who come in at the stations; and, if any one desires to be set down near his place of residence, he has only to mention it to the driver, and the train will be stopped to accommodate him. …

Elgin was a small place in Dr Johnson's time; but it is a busy bustling town now, with an extensive suburb of substantial mansions and neat villas, most of them embowered in luxuriant gardens blooming with flowers and teeming with fruit. It is the Cheltenham of the north.

After partaking of toddy from an ancestral tumbler – I wonder how many hogsheads of toddy that crystal goblet has held! I return to the train, and in less than half an hour plunge into the Highlands. It was shortly after he left Elgin that Dr Johnson made this entry in his diary: 'Here I first heard the Erse language.' I had heard the Ersc language before; but it was 'here' that I first heard it on this journey. It was not spoken; it was sung. The voice proceeded from a third-class carriage in my rear. By-and-by the strains were in front, and, as station after station was passed, the voice receded, and then came nearer again, which puzzled me not a little at first, but eventually explained itself in this way: a favourite singer of Erse [Scottish Gaelic] romances was in the train, and he was passing from carriage to carriage to give the third-class passengers a taste of his quality. As the Erse minstrel could not come to me, I went to him, and found him in the midst of a score of his fellows – apparently fishermen – singing as if for his life, while his auditors listened with open mouths and intense admiration. He sang song after song with a short dry cough at the end of each line, as a sort of vocal comma;

and as his audience never laughed, but preserved the most stolid gravity, I presumed that the lyrics were Homeric rather than Anacreontic. I must say that I felt rather ashamed, being a Scot born on the borders of the Highlands, to think that I did not understand a single word he sung. I thought to make some amends to myself by trying the Highlander with English; but that experiment only made the matter worse, for he not only understood English, but spoke it with remarkable accuracy. The popular idea in England is, that all Highlanders are red-headed. There were at least a hundred Highlanders in this train, and I did not notice more than three who were positively red. The majority of them were coal-black; and not one of them wore a kilt! The Erse language, when sung, sounds like German, and the native manner of singing is like the French. I bring an English lady in to see real Highlanders – she has only seen stage and snuff-shop-door specimens – and they stare at her so with their black eyes that she … escapes on the first opportunity. When the minstrel departs, I find that there is no Highlander left who can speak English. I cannot, therefore, make myself understood, until the happy thought occurs to me to express myself in whisky, when they all by a marvellous inspiration of intelligence comprehend me on the instant. My experience of life in all quarters of the globe leads me to believe that liquor is the language of the world.

Most appropriately the shades of night were falling upon the scene when the train, with a horrid scream, belching forth fire and smoke, rushed across the blasted heath near Forres. I really think the stoker got up the effect on purpose.

'WE SHALL BE BURNED ALIVE!'

ANONYMOUS ✦ 1866

*Before trains had corridors, passengers were
confined to their individual carriages*

WE WERE CLOSELY PACKED (in number, thirteen of us)
in the middle compartment of a second-class carriage on the
Midland line, some two years ago. Our carriage was the centre
carriage of a long train, and the compartments on either side
were empty. The journey, from Bedford to London, was express,
the pace near fifty miles an hour. We had stopped at only one
little station, and we were now off on a clear run of forty miles,
to be done in ten minutes under the hour, without stoppage. The
oil-lamp in the roof of the carriage, flickered pale and wan in the
broad daylight – for it was noontide – and in the glass cup
beneath, a spoonful of oil wagged and jogged and lurched about
with the motion. The company was monotonous and taciturn.
Being wedged in the middle of the seat between two gentlemen
of enormous proportions, where it was impossible to command
a window, I took to looking at this drop of wagging oil as the only
available object that kept time to the jolting and swaying and
clatter of the train. Although watching the drop of oil intently,
and noting the lively interest it seemed to evince in our progress
– leaping forward as we ran whish-sh past a station, or vibrating
as cr-r-r-sh-shoot we shot by another train – I was aware of the
wainscotted woodwork round it and the painted oak shingle that
seemed to dance and quiver with our motion. I saw it without
looking at it. What surprised and puzzled me, however, was this:
my eyes told me the pattern of the wainscot was changing. New
shingle seemed to rise up and swallow up the old, and then the
whole appeared to rise and fall in tiny waves. The solution my

mind suggested was, that I had biologised my sight, the oil-lamp serving as a disc.

My fellow-passengers began to talk. I heard them, my eyes were still fastened on the jolting drop of oil, which was beating time to a tune that engine, carriages, and rails, were playing in my head.

'Anybody smoking?' a deep voice said, snappishly. It seemed there was not.

'Then something is burning,' another voice said.

'It's only the guard putting the breaks on,' some one else explained.

I knew this was not so; our pace was unchanged; we had thirty more miles to run before the breaks would be put on. I saw why the pattern on the wainscot changed. The paint rose up in great blisters, and the smell of burning paint became powerful. The roof was on fire! Fearing to alarm the rest by an outcry, I momentarily scanned the faces of the passengers, who were loudly complaining of the smoke. I was trying to find a face that had a quiet spirit of help in it. I saw in the corner a calm-faced man of thirty, caught his eye, and pointed to the roof; for his was the only face in which I had confidence. I was right.

'Don't be alarmed,' he said, addressing the passengers and pointing, 'it is there—the lamp; it has just caught the woodwork a trifle; there is no danger; I am an engineer, and will stop the train.' Looking up, we all saw a brown-blistered cloud spreading over the roof, and heard the hissing and crackling of burning wood. The carriage quickly filled with smoke and became very hot; for the fire was fanned by a fifty-mile-an-hour blast.

'Do as I do,' the engineer-passenger called to me, flinging me his railway key.

I got to one door, and opened it, as he had done the other. Leaning out of the carriage, the engineer-passenger then gave a long shrill whistle, produced with two fingers against his teeth, harsh and grating almost as a railway whistle. I imitated him as I best could, and by incessantly slamming the doors on both sides we kept up such a tattoo as one would have thought could not fail to attract the attention of the guard, or the driver, or both. But five minutes passed, and we had not even made ourselves heard in the next carriage. Meantime tongues of fire were darting through the roof, and the volumes of hot pungent smoke became almost insupportable. The rest of the passengers appeared utterly bewildered; crouching together on the floor and against the draught of the doorways for air, feebly crying at intervals, 'We are on fire!' 'Fire!' 'We shall be burned alive!' Two wished to jump out and risk certain destruction rather than burning or suffocation; but we kept the doors.

The engineer made a good captain; he found them something to do. 'Use your voices, then,' he cried, 'shout away, but altogether. Now!' And every one shouted 'Fire!' with a will, and we resumed banging the doors. We had made ourselves heard at last in the next carriage, but the occupants were powerless to help us, and did not even know the cause of our dismay. As to communicating with the guard, it was simply hopeless. Ten minutes had gone since first we saw the roof blister. We had twenty good miles to run, and the daggers of flame were leaping far down from the roof. 'Don't be afraid,' said the engineer, 'if we can't get the guard to help us, we'll help ourselves.' He tied handkerchiefs to umbrellas and sticks, and gave them to two passengers to wave out of window to attract attention at the next station we shot past; some one might see our condition, and telegraph on to stop us by signal. At least, it would serve to keep the passengers quiet. Then he said, turning to me: 'Whatever is the cause of the fire, it is something *on* the roof, and not the roof itself. Will you climb the roof on one side, while I do the same the other? Only mind and get up to windward to clear the flames.'

We each set a foot on the door-rail, caught hold of the luggage-rod and swung ourselves up on the roof that was dashing along and pitching and tossing like a wild thing in a whirlwind. We could only kneel, for the rush of wind at the pace we were going would have carried us away had we stood up. The crash, the rattle, the swaying, the cutting draught, and the arches we shot through, that seemed to strike us on the head and make us cower down as we flashed by, the dazzling rails and the swift sleepers flying past in a giddy cloud, took my breath for the moment. But the engineer was busy cutting adrift, with his pocket-knife, a flaming pile of tarpaulins which the lamp had kindled, and which the wind was now drifting away in great pieces of fire along the line. I helped him with my knife and hands, and between us we quickly had the worst of the burning mass over in the six-foot way. The roof however was still burning badly, the fire eating out a large hole with red and angry edges that flickered fiercely in the draught. With the aid of bits of the unburnt tarpaulins, we managed to rub these edges and stifle and smother out the worst of the fire, until the occupants of the carriage had really very little to fear.

Whether the guard or engine-driver observed us on the carriage roof and so pulled up the train, or whether the handkerchief signals of distress were seen at some station whence the station master telegraphed to a signalman to stop the express, I never ascertained; but as soon as the fire was well-nigh subdued, the train slackened and stopped. And I well remember that while the officials were busily engaged in drenching the now empty carriage with buckets of water, a director, who happened to be in an adjoining carriage, very severely reprimanded us for what he told us was an indictable offence, namely, leaving a train in motion. As we stood there with blackened faces and black blistered hands, it scarcely occurred to us to make the obvious defence that, in an isolated compartment, without any possible means of communication with the guard, we had had no alternative but to choose between burning, and breaking the company's rules. I do not know the engineer-passenger, and I have never seen him since, or I would have exchanged congratulations with him on the company's having had the merciful consideration not to take proceedings against us.

CATCHING
FARE EVADERS

ANONYMOUS ✦ 1870s

A worker on the Manchester, Sheffield & Lincolnshire Railway (MS&L) describes measures taken against those less inclined to pay their way

IN THE VILLAGE of the station of the old MS&L. ... there were a number of miners, lime burners, boat men and farm hands who openly boasted that if they paid their train fare to the market town a few miles away they could come back without paying and so 'diddle' the Company. As this was an open bit of 'brag' both at street corners and in the tap room the whole station staff put their heads together to put the 'kybosh' on it, in other words to put a stop to it and make the boaster pay up. The 'dodge' was always practised on Saturday nights, when often as many as two hundred persons booked from our station. Some, however, did not book, but managed to rush onto the platform just as the train was about to start, saying they would pay at the other end. This our boss did not mind a bit because as the station staff at the 'far end' was ample and ... every possible exit was well looked after and managed by a foreman named Tom no one could get outside the station without giving a ticket or by paying. It was the late-coming passengers at our station who 'diddled' the MS&L...

It was a rather complicated job for it was usual for a number of men and women to get on at the far end of the platform to await the coming of the return train some hours later, and the 'diddles' were in the habit of mixing with this group until the chance of 'sliving' off by the rails at the end of the platform into the way leading to the village or round the end of the platform into the highway. A quarter of an hour before the train was due in, Jack, our nightman, and John, our platelayer, took hand lamps and casually inspected the group in waiting and spoke with several of the dozen or so and took particular note of them. Then John slung a shunting rope from the end post of the railings to the column of the water tank, not much of a barrier, but just enough to make a man stoop to get under and impossible to get over. Then John and Jack went a few yards up the siding and behind some wagons waited the train just due in. The station master stood at the way out while Bill looked after the other side and myself was at the little gate at the crossing. As the train steamed out it was seen that the group in waiting was very much larger, and our whole staff closed in on the lot and the station boss called upon the crowd to pay the fare from the market town. It was seen at once the whole party of the regular 'diddles' were trapped and when one began to shell out the few coppers due they all followed suit including some of the really waiting group urged on by John's loud spoken assurance that they were all known and would be summoned if they did not pay. The cap fitted even those who had not 'diddled' that time, and the lads were let off. As it was just before Christmas the haul was a good one and I was glad to see that one of my fellow lodgers had been caught, one of those who had bragged the most about 'doing' the MS&L.

It was noticed that the 'kybosh' we had put on was of some use for neither was the waiting group so large nor were the 'diddlers' so many and the bragging ceased altogether. Yet there will always be some who think it a fine feat to 'do' a railway company and the best way to thwart such is to put the 'kybosh' on when possible and by any means possible.

ONE DAY
IN BLACKPOOL

ANONYMOUS ✦ 1871

Railways opened up the possibility
of a day trip to the coast

WE RESOLVED TO make a ... journey to Blackpool, returning the same day – 2s. 6d. Twice forty nine, ninety eight miles; say 100 for the sake of the 'round numbers', for half-a-crown – three miles, like three sticks, a penny. Positively, if the fares get much further reduced, the pay will come from the other side; the companies will be giving us something to go, and it will be cheaper to travel than to stop at home!

Having provided ourselves with tickets we waited for the train, which drew up punctually to the platform. Some of the carriages with their contents had come from Oldham, others from Ashton and thereabouts, and a few were reserved empty for passengers by the way. We secured a seat among pleasant company in the latter half of the train. After several stoppages we arrived at Bolton, and took up more passengers. The Boltoners, indeed, appear to be a nomadic people. We were never at that dingy old timber and whitewash shed without exchanging one lot of travellers for another, and however good the advice to 'waken and see Bolton' may be, the Boltoners apply it to other places than their native town, and travel accordingly. Wherefore a *new* and clean station has just been built for them, and it is probable that they will travel still more. One doesn't see much of Bolton from the train, except the underground portion, from which it appears to be a benighted place. We soon get, however, to the open country, to Rivington Pike, and the level expanse of Horwich at its foot, soon to smoking Chorley, by pleasant Leyland, and across the wide Ribble to proud Preston. Whatever Preston may have to be proud of – it is not its railway station, but we don't stay long in it, for we are soon under way, and Fishergate and Preston, with its tall chimneys and taller spires, are left behind. At Poulton another train was hooked on to us, all third class, and no two carriages alike. Variety had evidently presided at their birth. Soon afterwards we glided up to the outside platform reserved for excursionists at Blackpool, after a journey of only ten minutes longer than that of the ordinary train.

But getting on to the platform and getting off it, except among the carriage wheels, were two different things. The late occupants of our train, and of two or three others that had immediately preceded it, nearly filled it, and the friends of the new arrivals come to meet them made circulation all but impossible. It was necessary to push our way through to get into the street, and there was a continuous stream of people along both sides of Talbot Road, all the way to the square of that ilk. Talbot Road has been very much improved within the last three or four years. The unsightly gaps have been filled up with good houses and shops, and the ramshackle old wooden sheds replaced by handsome buildings. Looking down this human avenue we saw before us the many-twinkling smile of ocean. The tide, not only of busy human life, but also of the sea, was at the full. There was a light air just sufficient to cause a ripple in the sunlight, and the sea, looked at from the road, seemed to rise like a brilliant wall before us … The promenade, as far as the eye could reach, was one long crowd. The pier was black with piers and pieresses, and the roadway was occupied by the open chariot of the period, charged with various solid masses of the genus excursionist. The Manchester variety, numerous as it had looked at the station, was lost in the countless throng. Halifax had sent, in one despatch, 'five hundred good as he' and there was, in short, a general gathering of the clan tripper.

There used to be a saying at Blackpool, that 'the trippers were caught by the wind as soon as they had turned the Clifton Arms corner, carried out to low-water and to South Shore, and were never again heard of'. No doubt, the shore, the cliffs, and the streets inland have great powers of absorption; but, the excursionist, this time, had it all his own way. He floated on the surface everywhere, buoyant and irrepressible ... the stick-merchant displayed his choicest wares – the photographer his unequalled and scowlingest portraits ... But the excursionist is wary, and though he may spend his money with, in some cases, not the best judgment in the world, he does not give voluntarily. He prefers to have something for his money. He certainly raised the flyman's fares. One of these wanted eighteenpence to take three passengers less than a quarter of a mile, and smilingly declined the proffered shilling, adding, 'you'll find no shilling fares today', which we subsequently found to be correct...

It was a Saturday that we were spending by these yellow sands, and on that day there arrives a special train freighted with a most precious and desired cargo – the husbands, brothers, and lovers of the fair toilers of the sea, who have been left disconsolate since the departure of the 8.20 train of the preceding Monday or Tuesday, as the case may be. The British matron brings her scarcely-to-be-controlled lads with the sea-and-sun-burnt cheeks to see the 'governor', or her girls, like the Trojan ladies, *crinibus passis*, but with happier reason. Ethel and Milly come to see what their brother George or Reginald has to say about them, and hope he is unaccompanied this time by that tiresome Fred. Juliet comes to see Arthur or 'Harry dear' by whom she is borne off, not unwillingly, in triumph and a fly. Long before the arrival of the train, the arrival platform has become the ground of a mutual admiration society. The girls have come to see, and, as we have heard it insinuated, to be seen also; and the youths, the proprietors of the shortest-skirted of coats, and of the Lilliputian-est walking sticks, wander, not unseen, until their noses are put out of joint by the arrival of the noon express. The staff at the Blackpool station appear to consist of one porter. He is civil, flustered, stout; wears, appropriately to the scene, sandy hair and has almost realised the impossibility that was alleged of Sir Boyle Roche's bird, the faculty of being in two places at once. What duties he doesn't do are discharged by the public and the engine-driver. The train at length arrived, after Juliet had worried herself through an eternity of two minutes. Paterfamilias pocketed the *Saturday* and permitted himself to be taken forcible possession of, the luggage was scrambled for, cars were driven dexterously over the flags, and Manchester was an affair of the past.

Since the morning a stiff breeze had sprung up, which made a walk on the pier a question of the continued proprietorship of our hat. So we adjourned for a refresher to the Clifton. There was Blackburn occupying the porch, Manchester in the person of the charming manageress in the hall, Manchester in the bar, and Manchester again entering as we left. A drive down to South Shore again, and an early cup of tea occupied the time till the clock struck the hour for returning. Blackpool wept at our departing, and so did several small children in our carriage, but we soon got into a more favoured climate, and reached Manchester in good time in the evening.

A Railway
Discovery

ANONYMOUS ✦ 1870s

*Some curious goings-on around a station on the
Manchester, Sheffield & Lincolnshire Railway*

THE SURROUNDINGS OF my first station and my last on
the old MS&L line were of a curiously varied nature, piles of
rammel out of disused ironstone pits one side, colliery refuse
hard by, a sand hole at the foot of the refuse, and over the way a
series of claypits full to the brim with water, and just beyond
a limestone quarry, all of which had some connexion with the
railroad or had either in building the line or its trade. The
ironstone had run out and did not pay; the coal pulleys still
revolved in the distance; fumes rose from the kilns, but clay
working had long ago died out. Altogether it was a rough looking
spot, and the level crossing close to the station buildings was a
silent and deserted place after dark. I mention this fact because
it has something to do with what I am about to relate, but before
I go on, I must digress somewhat, yet the pieces will fit in as you
will presently see.

At that time the whole countryside adjoining the line was by
no means a peaceful one. There were gypsy camps in every lane,
and on the common a mile away, and poachers were at work
every night with guns, pegs and nets. Poaching was almost a
recognised trade and was in a measure winked at not only by
cottage residents but by the thinly scattered police, whilst
gamekeepers were not altogether unfriendly to men wearing
coats in which were pockets big enough for game bags into which
no man might pry in danger of a split head. Foremen on farms,
constables, head keepers and others of the more substantial
workers were by no means averse to finding lying at their front or

back doors a brace of pheasants, a hare or two couples of rabbits on opening their doors in the morning. They were accepted and taken in by the finders, who knew the donors to be night-birds in the shape of poachers, who in this way bought silence and a shut eye to their night's doings. Gatehouse keepers were extremely favoured in respect of these gifts, for the way of the poacher was mostly over a lonely crossing, and when heavy loads were the result of a night's work it was easier to go through rather than over a gate, which at a certain signal would open magically. So too with the keepers of the game themselves on holdings where every kind of game were to be accounted for and actually counted up each evening and again in the morning by and for their owners. To keepers who were watched and their actions pried into by jealous owners the poachers' silent gifts were by no means unacceptable. And about this night work there hung a mystery, for when the poachers were watched and dogged in the night time the earth seemed to swallow them up when they reached a certain railway crossing gate.

At the station I was at, partly on and partly off the railway was a shed close by the goods warehouse into which the railway rubbish had been pitched for years to look at the heap, which looked like the remains of a 'pitch-in', for there were parts of engines, wagons, sleepers, chairs, lengths of rails, heaps in a delightful confusion. Our 'Boss' long had an eye on this assortment, and over and again decided he would have a hunt in the heap, why he did not say, but as he also had gifts of game left at his door the lumber shed perhaps gave him an idea. On a certain day when the sidings were clear and work slack he assembled all the staff, with John the linesman, and a start was made in the 'glory hole' as he called the shed. Some old sleepers and two or three old barrows were pulled away from the heap, and Jack the 'wild Irishman' saw there was a hole 'behint'. Down he went on his knee and felt about. 'Arrah,' he shouted, 'look out,' and he came out of the hole with a gun in his hand. 'Sure, the barls somewhere,' and in he went again. 'Faith, here's feathers', and this time he pulled out both feathers and gun, a brace of pheasants and a hare tied together, the hare 'nice and warum,' he said. There was no little excitement in the group, and Jack the platelayer said, 'Ah begin ter smell summat,' in his wise way. The Boss shouted, 'Pull some more stuff out,' and the hole was large enough for John to crawl in with the lighted stump of a signal candle in his hand. With a wild 'whoop' he shouted, 'Come on,' and in crawled all of us, and the candle light revealed a veritable 'robbers den' as ever described in boy's fiction. Three sides of the place were lined with upright old sleepers, in which were fixed large nails to act as hooks. From the nails dangled nets, pegs and bags, two of which were filled with freshly killed game of several kinds. In a tub were found a couple of ferrets, while a loaded gun was reared in another. In the roughest corner of the den was a sort of step-ladder leading upwards. This was the way out as well as into the 'den' over the rest of the pile of rubbish. On other nails were some coats and jackets which one of the party said he had seen before, outside the den with men inside them. Along one side of the floor was a pile of sacks and straw, which showed that the den was used as a sleeping room at times ... round the den were various things: a small hamper basket ... besides miscellaneous items of small value. The find made a considerable sensation at the time, and the 'den' was emptied. The hiding place was a clever one, much the same as found in a neighbouring wood a few years before. It also explained the sudden disappearance of the poachers, a gang of three only it was thought. It was surmised that when they reached the level crossing they entered the gate at the side then stooping ran along the metals below the level of the platform round the end of the shed platform and so unseen into the rubbish heap up which they scrabbled and so into the 'den' below.

A Trip on
an Incline

Anonymous • 1875

*A walk very quickly turns
into a perilous trip*

THE TRAMWAY AT the Brendan Mine is quite worth making
a trip to see. During a visit to West Somerset last autumn, we
made a journey thither. Having driven to the pretty little village
of Nettlecombe, we found that upwards of an hour would elapse
before any train started for the foot of the tramway, and as the
distance to it was under three miles, we – that is, myself and two
friends – decided upon walking.

Following the railway track, we walked through a lovely
wooded undulating country, and in close proximity to a rapid
stream, that leaped and rushed over and amongst boulders and
stones, indicating, by its equable distance below the railway, that
we were walking up a steep incline. From some considerable
experience in these matters, I am inclined to think the slope of
the railway was about one in forty. In less than an hour, we
reached a station at the foot of the tramway, and we then saw
what was before us. There, straight as an arrow, was a double
line of rails, pointing upwards at what my friends asserted was
nearly forty-five degrees, and extending above half a mile. So
steep did this slope appear, that even to walk up it would have
been work of great labour, and yet we were bound to ascend and
descend in a railway carriage, or rather truck. On the summit of
this incline, we could see some tiny objects moving round a large
square block of something that seemed to be in dangerous
proximity to the edge of this precipice, for such it looked.
Our binoculars revealed that the square block was a railway
truck, and the other objects were men who were hovering round

it. A railway porter at the station at the foot of the incline informed us that the length of this incline was fifty-two chains, and that the rise was one in four. Now, as the chain is twenty-two yards, the length of this tramway was eleven hundred and forty-four yards; and the rise in that distance being one in four, we found that we should rise eight hundred and fifty-eight feet during our journey, or rather more than twice the height of St Paul's, in less than three-quarters of a mile, and this, too, at railway speed. Having realised these facts, we began to speculate on the amount of risk we ran in this journey, and we examined the porter as regards accidents.

'Well, sir,' said the man, 'we can't well have an accident, because we turn the points so that if the rope broke, and the trucks broke loose, down they'd come, and be shunted off on the siding; and so they couldn't run down the line, and come in collision with anything. Once the rope did break, sir, and it was all settled here, close to the station.'

'How settled?'

'Why, the trucks just broke up, and spread the ore over the rail.'

'But how about the passengers?'

'There were none, sir, luckily; and so there was no harm done.'

We immediately proceeded to an examination of the rope by which the trucks were dragged up the incline. It was a wire-rope, and it looked fearfully small; but then we reflected upon the manner in which the traffic on this quaint railway was carried on, and we became more confident. The method was, that a wire-rope, rolling round a drum, was made fast to the trucks at the bottom and at the top of the tramway. Those at the top were filled with iron ore, and, by their extra weight, ran down the incline, and dragged up the empty carriages. Those which descended the incline full were soon emptied, and those at the top exchanged for full ones; so that the loaded trucks always descended, while the empty ones ascended. Thus there was not a very great strain upon the rope, and we felt quite prepared for the ascent.

In order to ascend the incline comfortably, a plank and some sacks were placed in the truck, and on these we seated ourselves, and before starting, noted the time, and that we were in a sort of basin surrounded by high hills. There is a sudden jerk as the rope that holds our truck becomes taut, and is stretching upwards; we hold on to the sides of the truck, for our seat seems insecure, and as though a very little would upset us. On moves the truck, very steadily now, but with increasing velocity. We look upwards, and there we see two or three loaded trucks rushing down towards us. We look back and downwards, but this is rather giddy work, and we don't like it; but when we look at the hill-tops behind us, a most curious effect is visible. So sudden is our rise, that the hill-tops that seemed to hang over us as we started are now depressed, whilst above them rise the Welsh hills, the Bristol Channel, and the intermediate country of North Somerset. So quickly does the scene change, and hill ascend above hill, that we can scarcely picture one scene before it is quickly superseded by another.

But suppose the rope broke? If it did so when we were ascending, we have our remedy. The truck, being no longer dragged up this steep incline, would suddenly stop, then descend, and with increasing velocity, until it came to that safe place below, which the porter had intimated would prevent an accident, by dashing the truck to pieces. There was an instant when, by presence of mind, we could escape without any danger; it was at the instant when the truck came to rest. At that second of time we could jump down, and calmly contemplate the headlong rush and destruction of the truck in its descent. But how about our going down? If the rope then broke, this expedient could not be put into practice, for there would be a sudden increase of speed, and no instant of time when we could jump down with safety. These thoughts passed rapidly through my mind, for we had only gone half-way up the incline, when the down-trucks rushed past us with a groan and a whiz, that added to our giddiness. And lo! upon one of these trucks sat a little girl about seven years old, who seemed as much at home in rushing down that incline, as she would be on her mother's knee. I glanced round at my two companions, who had, during the last few seconds, become very quiet. Our eyes met, and one of my friends remarked what a lovely view it was. As I regarded him, I knew he was playing a false card; his lips were tightly set, and the clutch of his hands on the truck was such that I could see the muscles standing out on their backs, and I knew that, however much my companions might command their feelings, yet they were unmistakably dismayed. But at length our truck suddenly came to a stop: we had ascended eight hundred and fifty-eight feet in vertical height, during what appeared to us a very long time; but, on referring to our watches, we found it was only three minutes and fifty-six seconds from the time of leaving the lower to reaching the upper station; and we were assured that, if we had walked it, we could not have accomplished the distance under eighteen minutes.

The view from the summit of this tramway is well worth the rush up and down. The locality on which we stood must have been upwards of twelve hundred feet above the sea-level, and the extent of country visible was immense. South Wales, the Bristol Channel, Exmoor, Dartmoor, Wiltshire, South Dorset, were all visible; and had the day been clearer, we should have had a more distinct view of the farthest ranges in Devon and Cornwall. But our time was short, for if we did not return by the next down train, we should be detained for more than two hours; so, having seated ourselves on some sacks placed on the ore with which the truck was loaded, we turned our backs to the descent, and resigned ourselves to our fate.

I can quite understand that if a man went up and down this incline every day, he would soon be able to read his *Times*, whilst thus raised and lowered, with as much ease and comfort as people now do when travelling express on an average railway; but we were not accustomed to it. I do not hesitate to confess that a curious feeling – a sort of mixture of giddiness, sea-sickness, and uncertainty – took possession of me, as we felt ourselves rushing down this steep incline, now on a level with a tree-top; an instant after, far below its roots. Then, as we looked down far beneath us in the distance, we could see that very careful porter standing at the foot of the incline, having no doubt turned the points so as to cause the trucks to dash themselves to pieces close to his home, and thus, as he termed it, to prevent an accident. But I would rather have travelled a little farther, in the hope that we might find some reduction of the speed, enough to enable us to jump off from our Mazeppa-like position.

We, however, reached the foot of the incline in safety, and by the aid of a ladder, descended to the ground, whence we stepped into a comfortable first-class carriage, and once more travelled in a manner to which we had been accustomed, and which was less trying to our nerves than that rush up and down eight hundred and fifty-eight feet in less than four minutes.

'It was well worth the journey to go up and down that incline,' remarked our host, when we were seated that evening quietly after a good dinner.

'Oh, certainly,' replied one of our companions; 'but, to tell you the truth, it was rather nervous work.'

'And to think, after all,' I remarked, 'that the inclination of the slope was only fourteen degrees!'

'Fourteen degrees? Nonsense!' was the reply; 'It must have been nearer forty-five.'

A demonstration, however, convinced our companions that they had committed the common error of over-estimating a slope; for the fact is, that a rise of eight hundred and fifty-eight feet in about eleven hundred and fifty yards gives an angle of about fourteen degrees. It was enough!

THE SHUNTER:
A CHAPTER FROM REAL LIFE

WALTER HUDSON ✦ 1880s

The MP for Newcastle upon Tyne, writing in 1916, recalls his life as a shunter twenty-five years previously

IT WAS ONE NIGHT when I was a shunter on the North-Eastern railway at Darlington. There was a howling hurricane and the rain came down in torrents. Traffic was greatly delayed, and the driver of a goods train I had to make up was in a hurry to get away. The deafening roar of the wind drowned every shout, and my lamp had blown out; so that I was unable to communicate clearly by sign or sound with the engine-driver. And you must remember that in those days we had not even the coupling-pole in use, and the shunting yards were not lighted like so many of them are to-day. I had coupled the first truck to the engine, and was just coming from between the buffers ready to give the 'right-away' signal, when to my horror the engine started, and I was knocked down in the four-foot way. I shall never forget the horrors of the next few minutes. The mere memory of it causes cold shivers to run down my back to this day. There were over forty waggons, and with a grinding, roaring noise they rolled above me, first slowly then more rapidly, until, helplessly placed as I was, the noise became maddening. I had the presence of mind to lie lengthwise and as flat as possible.

But even now I recall how two possibilities flashed across my mind and drove me almost frantic with fear. One was that a coupling chain might reach down and strike my head; and in my nervous excitement I put my hands at the back of my head to act as a shield. And then I remembered that there was an engine at the other end of the train, which would have to run out after the train had left to go to the sheds for the night. Of course I knew that it could not pass the points until the train had cleared, as it had to be switched on to a different line. I was lying about thirty yards from the points. Would the engine run over me or not before stopping to wait for the points to be opened? If it did it meant almost certain death. If it did not, I should have time to jump up before the points were open. Seconds seemed like hours. Suddenly I could hear the panting engine above the din and the thunder of the storm and the roar of the passing trucks. Closer and closer it came, and louder came the fearful noise. I was almost frenzied with fear. So near came the sound that I had resigned myself to being killed. But in a flash the rattle of the trucks above me stopped, and the panting gave place to the hiss of escaping steam about ten yards away from me. I was saved; and as I jumped up and out, I really shouted with joy, so keen was the relief. Soon after that I gave up shunting and became an assistant guard.

A Trip on the Footplate

Rev. V L Whitechurch + late 1890s

*A reverend recounts his experiences on the footplate
on a train from London Bridge to Portsmouth*

NO ONE KNOWS what railway travelling really is until he has stood on the footplate of a locomotive, his iron steed darting ahead at the rate of a mile a minute. The passenger in his comfortable padded seat knows little as he skims his paper, glances at the surrounding scenery, hears the prolonged shriek of the whistle, or feels the grinding of the brake, of the two men at work in front of him, two men black and greasy with coal dust and oil, who hold in their hands and steady brains the power and knowledge that enable them to drive their load of precious human freight over the iron road.

Owing to the kindness of the Locomotive Superintendent of the London, Brighton and South Coast Railway, I was privileged, some time since, to take a run on one of his fine new four-wheels coupled bogic engines drawing an express from London Bridge to Portsmouth. The driver, an old veteran of forty years' 'running', greeted me warmly as I stepped aboard, motioning me to stand on the right side of the 'cab', so as to be as little in the way as possible, the driver on this line always standing on the left. I buttoned my coat and put on a cap, making myself snug for the journey; a shrill whistle sounded somewhere back on the platform, the driver opened the regulator, the great engine began to glide forward, and we were off with a run of seventy odd miles in front of us before we were scheduled to pull up.

Leaving London Bridge Station, with its maze of points and cross roads, behind, we were soon bowling merrily along with the coast clear ahead. The driver had 'notched her up'; that is to say he had taken a few turns with the 'reversing wheel' (the wheel is universally supplanting the old lever and notched quadrant of the reversing gear), so that the rush of steam into the cylinders was 'cut off' after part of the stroke, the object being both to economise and to expand the steam – it also prevents much resistance of used steam on the other side of the piston on the return stroke. The fireman, meanwhile, was taking a look at his gauge-glass, the indicated pressure of which was rapidly rising to one hundred and seventy pounds pressure on the square inch, the 'working pressure' and 'blowing-off point' of our engine.

And here let me mention that it is by no means the fireman's duty merely to shovel on coals. He has a great deal more to think about than that. In the first place 'coaling' itself is a very skilful operation, the secret being to distribute the coal equally in the fire box and to keep the shape of the fire therein concave. Then he has to keep up a uniform pressure of steam and this is only done by watching the gauge-glass attentively, by coaling frequently and not much at a time, and by opening the 'damper' when an ominous hissing white cloud, coming from the safety valve, shows that 'she's blowing off'. Besides all this, a certain amount of coal is allowed for the trip. If this is exceeded there is a 'fine'; if on the other hand, less is used, it goes towards a 'premium'. A strong lesson in practical economy is it, therefore, to watch the fireman's work while the engine is running.

A good speed was soon attained as we flew through the stations, and a shaking, rocking motion as the iron steed leaped ahead. The noise was deafening, a constant thudding with a 'bang, bang' like the report of a pistol at times as we 'took' the points at the various junctions. I use the expression 'jumping forward' advisedly, for one of the strangest experiences to a novice is the feeling that the engine every now and then appears to *jump* upward and forward, doubtless due to a certain amount of oscillation on the springs. Another curious sensation is the view of the road ahead. You look through the 'weather glass' adown the great boiler, beyond the snorting 'smoke jack', and see the glint of the metals converging to a distant point, and seem to feel that the track with its adjacent hedges or buildings is rushing on to you with a force that must end in overwhelming destruction.

'Hold on, sir!' came as a note of warning from the old driver, as he drew the old regulator over to 'shut', and laid his other hand on the little handle of the cock of the 'Westinghouse brake', that most wonderful invention which brakes the wheels all along the train by means of compressed air pumped into a reservoir on the engine as we hasten along, and conveyed thence by means of the familiar coupled pipe to cylinders beneath the carriages.

We were about to round the sharp curve going into Mitcham Junction. A glimpse of a large board by the side of the track with a 'Reduce speed' warning, a sharp *hiss* as the air rushed out of the pipes, a lurch over to the left and a grinding noise as the brakes go on, and a hasty clutch on my part at the edge of the cab to keep myself from falling. The driver gave me a grin and a few reminiscences about this particular curve, and we were off again, flying past the signal-posts with the red warning arm lowered to 'safety', all carefully noted by the driver and his mate with their eagle eyes – eagle, indeed, to be able to pick the particular arm they want out of a forest of semaphores that arises at a big junction, or to tell by night the particular spark of 'green' in the maze of lights that flashed the signal for them to 'Go ahead'. No wonder the companies impose severe 'sight tests' on their drivers.

'Ha!' growled the fireman as we neared Sutton while the driver shut off steam. A 'bit of stick', the notched arm of a 'distant signal', was stretched out horizontally against us, a warning that the 'home signal' beyond likewise barred our way. We commenced to slow down, but at the same moment down went the obstructing arm, opened was our regulator, and in a few seconds we had flown through Sutton and were bowling away on the straight bit of line beyond. Presently we approached a falling gradient. This presents a curious effect from the footplate. The level line before it seems to end abruptly with a dip over a precipice beyond, and it appears that you *must* be on the point of being hurled to destruction.

Epsom, with its two stations and terrific curve, was passed with a warning whistle and many a hiss of the brake, and we plunged shortly into the magnificent scenery beyond

Leatherhead. Another sharp curve, a towering mass of hills in front of us with the gleaming metals leading to a smoke-begrimed opening – a shriek as of despair at entering the mouth of the tomb, and we plunged into the darkness of the tunnel. The sensation now became very curious, the rushing and roaring of the air at our sides as we cleft our way through it, and away beyond a little round hole of light growing larger every moment. I thought of the time when this same Dorking Tunnel had fallen in, and imagined the awful feeling that would ensue if that little spark of light became suddenly blocked.

Out into the open country, and we were the other side of the North Downs. The driver gave a sweep of his arm behind to call my attention to the lovely scenery. Then we scudded through woods, around curves, over embankments, down cuttings, and the veteran turned to me and said: 'Pretty road, isn't it? Ah, I know it well. Many's the time I've come down here in a pitch black night when you couldn't see a yard on the track ahead, in all sorts of weathers, rain, wind – the bitter cold when you're almost frozen behind as the draught sweeps in, the blinding snow, when your weather – glass gets clogged and you have to put your head out over the side of the cab to catch sight of your signals. It's no child's play, is a driver's work, sir, and there's few think of the responsibilities of it either.'

A signal against us, and we stopped dead for a minute or two. We could hear impatient passengers behind us pulling down the windows to look out. The driver glanced at his watch; we were getting a bit late.

'Never mind,' he said, 'we've got the best of the run before us yet. Ah! off we go!' and the good iron horse snorted as the steam once more rushed into her cylinders. Horsham was passed in fine style, and a mile or so beyond the driver pitched out a folded newspaper as we tore by a signal box. 'It's a lonesome bit o' duty there,' he explained, 'and they're glad of something to read.'

This was one of the many kindly little acts on the line of men who, perhaps, never get the chance of speaking to one another from year's end to year's end.

The pace increased, and the half-way point, Billingshurst, could hardly be discerned as we went through. Twilight was beginning to close in and the faint glimmer of green lamps ahead told us that the signalmen were alive to the growing darkness. We approached Pulborough and I consulted my watch.

'More than five minutes late by your scheduled time,' I remarked.

The driver grinned once more as we ran out into the open and level plain beyond.

'Now,' he said, 'here's where I make my running, and you'll see what driving is.'

I stepped back out of the way and hung on as best I could while the fireman shovelled more coals into the roaring furnace. When I got back to my place the driver produced his tea tin and offered me some refreshments. The engine had kept it warm. A novel situation for 'afternoon tea' is the footplate of an engine, especially when she's doing close to fifty miles an hour. That was our rate as we dashed through Amberley, through the little tunnel beyond, until Arundel Castle showed up grimly against the darkening sky on our right. A flash of a row of lamps, and we run through Arundel Station. Beyond us was a tremendous curve, where the 'Mid Sussex', on which we were running, joins the 'South Coast' portion of the line. With his regulator closed and his hand on the brake-handle, the steady old driver peered ahead. 'Hiss! Cr-r-r-r!' and I grasped the edge of the cab once more with all my might. 'Bang-bang!' we thundered over the crossing points with a jolt and a rattle, our pace now but a slow one. A minute more time and the Arun was crossed and we ran through Ford Junction.

'Now time us,' said the driver as he threw open the regulator, and I took my watch and noted the time … from Ford to Chichester is a run almost as straight as an arrow and almost dead level, the distance being about ten miles. We did this bit of the run at the rate of sixty miles an hour, and in parts of it this speed was increased, but, owing to the nature of the road, we did not seem to be going nearly as fast, so much easier was the motion. It was quite dark now, and soon a glare of lights ahead warned us that we were approaching our first stopping-place, Chichester. Full half-a-mile before we arrived there, the driver shut off steam, and we ran in with our own impetus, the fireman screwing down the hand-brake while his companion applied the vacuum, stopping to a nicety at the end of the platform.

'What's the time?' asked the driver.

'We're a minute early,' I said, consulting my watch.

'Told you we'd make it up, sir,' he replied with a chuckle; 'we did that last bit in fine style, didn't we?'

'Right away.'

'Snort-snort', and we were off once more into the darkness of the night, our destination being Portsmouth. Many a friendly green light flashed before us from time to time as we sped along with roar and thunder. The fireman was resting very soon now – saving his last shovelful of coals. The furnace was dying down from its leaping flames into red embers, the tell-tale hand on the steam-gauge glass was going gradually back and back. The iron horse was preparing for his rest – to be preceded by a good 'rubbing down' when his master 'signed off' and delivered him into the hands of the 'cleaners' at the terminus shed. A stop at Fratton for the collection of tickets. A few minutes more and Portsmouth Town was reached, and shaking the honest hands of the trusty driver and his mate I bade them good-night after an exciting and thoroughly enjoyable two hours with them 'on the footplate'.

DRIVING
THE QUEEN

ANONYMOUS ✦ 1890s

*An engine driver explains the various gratuities
on offer for performing his duties*

EVERY TIME I TAKE Her Majesty across the sleepers
I receive, on the following pay-day, a bonus equivalent to half a
week's wages. I can't say for certain whether it is a gratuity from
the Queen, but I'm inclined to think not. From what I can learn
it is given by the company, who in their turn are paid for these
special runs at the rate of 7s. 6d. per mile in addition to first-class
fares for each member of the Royal Family and suite. I have
already conveyed the Queen over my section of the line for ten
years without the slightest hitch, but it's an anxious time for me
as well as for the other officers.

A very unexpected gratuity was the one I got from an
Army officer. Having by just a few minutes missed the express
that was to land him at headquarters at the termination of
his furlough, he hurriedly, and at considerable cost, ordered
out a special; and being engaged shunting about the station
at the time, I was put on to the job. A short space of time
sufficed to attach the engine to a carriage and brake-van, and
off we started with the belated warrior, in hot pursuit of his
train. Up hill and down dale we tore along, unfettered by
schedule-time, and scattering showers of glowing coal from the
funnel. Eventually, and by the aid of the telegraph, the express
was overtaken at a large station some forty miles distance, and
I felt sufficiently rewarded by the success of my efforts, but was
still further gratified by the receipt through my foreman of a
letter of profuse thanks, enclosing a crisp five-pound Bank of
England charmer.

I have made a good many emergency stops – more or less quick – in my day, but none quicker or more satisfactory than the one that brought me the largest gift I ever received. We were running the night mail along the coast line at, I should say, fully fifty miles an hour, in a cutting made in the rocks, which, indeed, descended precipitously from a foot or two from the side of the rails. Immediately after rounding a sharp bend there loomed into sight an obstruction on the line a very short distance in front, and if I hadn't instantly put the brakes hard on, I shudder to think what the result might have been. As it was, the passengers, most of whom had been asleep, experienced a severe jolt, which, however, they thankfully excused on realising how narrow had been their escape. A spontaneous subscription was there and then made, and the proceeds presented to me. The obstruction turned out to be a huge log of timber which had fallen off the last train that passed in the opposite direction, and lay right in our path.

The gratuity on which I place most reliance, however, is the £5 premium which our company gives drivers for each complete twelve months they manage to run their trains without (to quote the wording of the condition) *causing, contributing to, or by neglect failing to prevent an accident to person or property*. I have received this for the matter of eleven years, and, if all goes well for a month to come, I shall have competed a further year.

FINES AND
REWARDS

ANONYMOUS ✦ 1890s

The chief of a London railway explains how
a worker can make his way in the railway

IF OUR ENGINES make much smoke when they are standing
in the open here, we have complaints from the police and the
neighbours. It is perfectly possible to prevent such a nuisance, for
a man has only to turn on his steam-blast and to open his
furnace-door. If he will not do so simple a thing we fine him. We
are bound to do that in self-protection ... Some lines fine a man
who is late in the yard or late with his engine out of it. Some fine
him for skidding the wheels of his train with the brake, or for
smoking on duty. The latter point is a case of pure discipline.
Given a dark, cold night, and an express travelling sixty mile an
hour, and inspector may be a little blind. But we could not have
drivers smoking about our stations for obvious reasons.

There are cases where a man can earn money by saving coal
consistently. Each class of engine is allowed so much coal per
mile. This amount varies with different lines from twenty-eight
to thirty-six pounds. Heavy goods engines require the larger
allowance – slow passenger engines the smaller. An account is
kept of the coal delivered to each man, and if he saves on his
allowance, he may earn promotion at the end of the year. You
must remember, too, that this work is very well paid. Drivers
earn from forty-two shillings to sixty-three shillings a week. Few
of our men work more than ten hours a day, and there are all
sorts of clubs for their benefit. Of course, they are skilled in
every sense of the word, and they have spent many years in our
service before they are given such responsible positions. Very few
drivers, even of goods trains, are less than thirty years old. Most

of our express men are over fifty. They begin by going into the sheds when mere lads, and there they learn all about an engine and how to clean it. Four or five years of cleaners' work promote them to the footplate of a goods engine as firemen. The next step is to the footplate of a slow passenger engine; after that, they become firemen to an express. It is now time to make drivers of them, and they go back, as it were, to the bottom of the ladder, beginning by driving a goods engine, then getting promoted to a slow passenger, and finally, when they are ripe with long experience, to the commanding position – driver of an express. Taken as a whole, a finer, more sober, steadier body of men does not exist. And I think you can say that for the drivers of every company in the country.

A Day in the Life of a Driver

Anonymous + 1890s

An engine driver out of Paddington explains his day

SUPPOSE I COME on to drive the ten-fifteen out of Paddington in the morning, I've got to be on my engine one hour at least before start. I'm generally on an hour and a quarter, but that's my look-out. If I take that train, I'll have, maybe, pretty well three hours to get my dinner and oil-up at Bristol; and I'll be back in the yard at Westbourne Park about half-past six. But my day is not done then by a long way. Before I can sign off I must take the old girl into the yard to the coal-shed, and see that she is coaled and watered ready for the next day. More than that, I must write up my report of the day's run and overhaul my engine from buffer to buffer, making a note of any little repair that may want doing. Generally speaking, sir, this company does not work us more than ten hours a day; though, of course, if a man's on a goods engine and is blocked on the road, he may be on his footplate for fifteen hours together. If that's the case, and he is locked up in a country siding after fifteen hours' work, he has the right to leave his train and run back to the nearest engine-shed for twelve hours' rest. We don't get much of that sort of thing since we've had four roads; and, all round, those four roads are a godsend. It lets we on the expresses drive with fewer checks, and it gives goods drivers a fair chance to do their journey…

A good driver must have his eyes on three thing at once, sir. He must look forward, so to speak, and yet keep his eye on the gauges and the furnace. It don't do for him to think as he's a mucky shepherd playin' at chuck halfpenny under a tree. There's hundreds of lives depending on his eyes, and he isn't to forget it either. You can't stop an engine going sixty miles an hour like you can stop a cab. She wants something to hold her, she does. That's where the strain comes in. A man must never think of anything but his train until he's pulled up at Paddington … There's as much difference between drivers as between carpenters. One man will give you sixty miles an hour with his gauge low; another won't drive fifty-five, and will be scooping up the coal half the time. An engine wants coaxing. She's just like a woman. You've got to know her, and to study her fancies.

MY LIFE
IN RAILWAYS

THOMAS HIGGS + 1890s

The chief assistant to the superintendent at
Swindon looks back to his days as a driver

I HAVE THE superintendence of the engines, the enginemen, firemen, cleaners, coalmen, and everything connected with the running department. I commenced my career on the London and North-Western Railway at Rugby in 1846, as office and bar-boy. I worked through the sheds and fitting shops until 1853. Then I commenced on the road as a fireman, and worked in that position until 1854, when I retired from the service of the London and North-Western Railway. After a short turn on the South Staffordshire Railway, and then some months in Dublin and Belfast, I joined the service of the London and South-Western Railway in 1856 as a fireman, and in the following year was promoted to the position of relief driver on the Dorset and Weymouth line. The same year I was made engine man, working on different parts of the railroad, running goods and passenger trains. Finally, in 1859, I settled at Salisbury, running between Salisbury and London. On the opening of the Exeter line I was shifted to Exeter, and then ran between Exeter and Salisbury. After that I was promoted to the express running between Exeter and London, up one day and down the next. That position I held until the 8th of July, 1868, when I was appointed locomotive foreman for Exeter, having in addition the supervision of all the signals and the gas and carriage departments from Yeovil to Bideford. In 1872 I was appointed district chief foreman for the Western District, from Basingstoke to all stations in the West of England. Ten years later I was removed from Exeter to London to take charge of the running department of the London and South-Western Railway, which position I have held ever since. …

I have never met with any serious accident, but was once scalded very severely in the execution of my duties. It occurred in October, 1862, and was caused by the heating apparatus giving out. I was laid up for five or six months. In 1863, a man attempted to throw me off the road with the mails coming over the North Devon line from Bideford to Exeter. Fortunately I managed to bring the train to a stand before any serious result occurred. Had I not stopped the train when I did, it would have been precipitated through a bridge into a river. …

He took a gate off its hinges and laid it across the road. Fortunately I saw him and pulled up in time. When he perceived that he was discovered, he ran away across the fields. I got down from my engine, and chased and caught him. He tried hard to get away; but I brought him to my engine, and carried him on to Crediton, where I handed him over to the police. I afterwards gave evidence against him at Exeter, and he was sentenced to five years' penal servitude … For my conduct on that occasion our directors gave me a silver medal and five pounds.

I have been rewarded on several occasions for preventing accidents and serious loss of life. I am happy to say that, during all my career, I have had to attend but one inquest on a person run over. This was at a level crossing. I never broke down on the road but twice. Once I broke the driving axle on an engine called the 'St George', but managed to bring the train on to the next station. I broke down once afterwards on the Exeter line. During all my career I have never travelled in a train where the engine has failed; and I have never at any time been travelling in a railway train where anything has gone wrong with the train.

As the engine has been improved, his position has been improved, too. A major consideration now, in constructing an engine, is the comfort of the driver. When I first went on to an engine there was nothing but a small hand-rail to prevent the men from falling off the footplate. There was nothing like the present protecting plates or cabs for the comfort of the men. …

Whenever Her Majesty travels on our line, I go on the engine. You see, it is necessary for someone to be on the train who would know what to do in case anything went wrong. One can never foresee what might take place, especially on a line like that from Windsor to Gosport, between which places there are no fewer than fourteen or fifteen junctions. The best run I ever did with Royalty on board was early last year, when we fetched the Prince and Princess of Wales from Wimborne. When I left London there was a dense fog. The Prince asked me what the weather was like in London. I said if there proved to be as much fog on the way as I had left in London, we should arrive two or three hours late. As a matter of fact, we found the fog in patches – here and there very dense, while here and there we found it quite clear. Whenever we got into the fog we had to crawl along, feeling our way and going along very cautiously; but as soon as ever we got a hit of clear daylight, I made her waltz along. Once or twice I put her to sixty-five miles an hour. When we reached Waterloo the finger was just on the point of twelve: we had done the journey to the minute. Our general manager was very pleased at the splendid run we had made, and so was the Prince.

Two
Accidents

WILLIAM LAWRENCE + 1890s

A former engine driver on the Great Western Railway, since pensioned off through ill health, recounts the accidents he has experienced

I BEGAN ON the Great Western in 1839, at Maidenhead. I then migrated to Twyford, where I was fitter's assistant. I subsequently became fireman and then driver. I joined the South Western in 1849, and ran from Nine Elms to Southampton with goods. Was advanced to the passenger work in 1851. In the month of November that year I was transferred to Twickenham, and ran from Twickenham to London and Windsor. In 1856 I came from Twickenham to Windsor, and continued to run betwixt here and London until 1881, when I met with a serious accident from a collision between Wraysbury and Datchet, which occurred on the 18th of January in that year.

Two trains were snowed up between Wraysbury and Datchet, and they telegraphed to Windsor for help. I and my mate were sent on with our engine. When we got to Wraysbury we did not know whether to go on or not, and so waited for information. In the meantime four engines had come up from London and had worked their way through, and not knowing I was on the line they ran smash into me. My mate had got off the engine and had asked me for the shovel. He wanted to keep himself warm by shovelling away the snow. Suddenly he says, 'Look out, mate!' But before I knowed where I was, the engines had struck my engine. I was knocked down and my left leg broken. The engine was sent along for some distance by the concussion. Then it stopped, and the engines struck it again. I was banged about once more, and half the coals in the tender heaped upon me. I had my senses all the time, and knew what was going on, but

I was pretty well done for. My left leg was broken in two places, my right hip was put out, my jaw was broken, and I was otherwise hurt. I was in the hospital a long time … I'm able to get about a bit, but I think I should have been all right, and able to go about my work, but for the hip being put out. …

I was in a rather serious one in 1859 or '60. It occurred to the 11.25 train from here (Windsor), between Ashford and Feltham. The rails had come away from the sleepers, and we ran right into a wheat-field, the train turning upon its side on a hedge. When I felt the engine going I jumped right over the fireman. He followed suit. When we found ourselves on the ground my mate says to me, says he, 'Bill, are you hurt?' I says, 'No, I'm not hurt, mate. Are you?' 'No,' says he; 'so let's thank God that neither of us is hurt.' Then he suggested that we should go and look at the train and see if anybody was injured. We peeped down the funnels to see who was in the carriages. There weren't many passengers in the train. But there was an old lady in a first-class compartment, along with a little girl, who was screaming and making a great hullabaloo. So we fetched assistance and set to work to get them out. But it wasn't an easy matter, for the train was on its side, and the carriage door was locked. Howsomdevers, we got the window open, and soon had the little girl out all right. But it was quite a different affair with the old girl, for she was eighteen stone if a pound. After considering a bit, my mate gets in through the window and tells the old lady to mount on the arm of one of the seats. Then he gives her a bump up behind, and me and another as we got to help us pulls up above, and presently, him thrusting and us pulling, we brought her out safe and sound. But it was a tough bit of work, and for a time it seemed as though she was going to stick, half-way in and half-way out. She was a good deal frightened, but not hurt; neither was anybody else in the train.

Yes, I have been able to do nothing since [1881] … and the company has very kindly looked after me.

ON LEAPING FROM LOCOMOTIVES

'A DRIVER' ✦ 1890s–1900s

An engine driver recounts
some of his near misses

MANY MIRACULOUS ESCAPES have occurred on our railways by enginemen taking a leap for life from their moving engines, although to outsiders it does seem at the first glance to be a case of 'out of the frying-pan into the fire'. I have come across a good many remarkable instances of this kind in my thirty-five years' experience of life on the iron road … and have myself passed through the critical ordeal without being any the worse, though my fireman on that memorable occasion unfortunately lost a leg by not following my example. We were working a night goods train, and after having backed into a siding at one of the stations to leave off some trucks and take on others, we were rejoining the main line, when just at that moment the midnight mail came thundering along.

I had only time to reverse my engine, whistle fiercely, and give her more steam to back off the road, when I saw as plain as day that all was up – we shouldn't be able to clear away in time. I immediately leapt off, and told my mate to follow; but he hesitated and was lost – at least his right leg was – as it was terrible jammed by the mail engine, which almost cut ours in two and overturned it into the bargain. Luckily, only a few of the passengers were affected, and those were but slightly shaken; but the signalman's momentary forgetfulness cost him his job.

I remember in my younger days a locomotive ran off from our yard. The only occupant was a venturesome clerk, who, in timorously leaping off, turned a complete somersault and alighted on his feet; the engine eventually stopping…

On another occasion a wheel tyre of one of our engines running a quick coal train burst with a tremendous bang. Almost simultaneously the locomotive gave an uncomfortable lurch, at which the alert driver sprang off and frantically dragged his fireman with him at the very instant that the ponderous engine, propelled by its own impetus and the momentum of the trucks behind it, toppled over the side of a thirty-feet embankment and fell in a heap into the field below. Of course, it and a half dozen of the loaded waggons which followed were much damaged – the latter, indeed, being smashed to atoms – and it would certainly have gone hard with the enginemen had they stuck to their posts.

A year or two ago one of our passenger trains connecting with a steam packet was gaily nearing the seaside terminus, which is approached by a moderate descent, when the driver, with dismay, found that his brake was failing to properly apply the blocks to the wheels, which, in consequence of the excessively slippery state of the rails by the deposit of brine from the sea, only revolved the faster.

By this time the train was just nearing the platform, on to which the terrified engineman leapt a second or two before the engine crashed into the stop-buffers and demolished the adjoining newspaper-stall; the front brake-van – fortunately empty – being forced over the tender and onto the footplate of the locomotive. The passengers entirely escaped, and the driver and fireman sustained but trifling bruises; but next morning the driver awakened to find that his hair had perceptibly whitened. As he subsequently explained, 'It wasn't the fright I got in jumping that did it, but the awful fear that some of the passengers might be killed.'

You know there are still such things as runaway trains – that is to say, goods trains that split up into two or more portions by a coupling snapping, the detached portion either stopping of its own accord or bolting right back afterwards, according to the presence or absence of gradients. Well, a runaway case occurred not long ago on our system, and the derelict portion took neither of the expected courses. After breaking away it had continued its original course slowly for a while, but soon encountered a steep-falling gradient, down which it rushed in the direction of the front part of the train. The driver and his mate saw what was about to happen, and wisely vacated their steed, thus avoiding serious injury.

I could tell of many more cases having both happy and unhappy terminations – instances of lives lost in leaping, and others lost through not leaping. The fact is, that just as there is a time for everything, so there is a time for leaping from locomotives. To be successful it must be done at the right moment and in the right direction – for there is a good deal in the choosing of the spot for the hurried exit.

As to the morality of the proceeding, well, I never knew of that being questioned. Drivers have the gift of being able to take in a critical situation at a glance, and instantly utilising their best resources. Until then they never think of deserting their post. But human life is ever more precious than railway rolling-stock.

SIGNIFICANT
EVENTS

1900–1948

By the early 20th century, railway building in Britain had virtually come to a halt. Controlled mainly by a few large and profitable companies, the rail network had reached its zenith. The Edwardian era also brought previously unheard of travel opportunities for well-healed travellers seeking to explore the Continent and beyond.

The First World War saw Britain's railways brought under Government control for the first time; they were soon carrying men and materials to Channel ports for onward shipping to the front line. In the reverse direction came ambulance trains and homeless refugees. By the end of the war Britain's railways were suffering from labour unrest and were in a rundown state. In 1923, they were grouped into the 'Big Four' regional companies. The Great Western Railway (GWR), London & North Eastern Railway (LNER), London, Midland and Scottish Railway (LMS) and Southern Railway (SR) not only went on to battle with increasing competition from road transport and the 1926 General Strike, but also succeeded in forging a golden age of rail travel until this was ended by the Second World War.

Once again the Government took control and, despite the best efforts of the Luftwaffe, the overstretched railways played a key role in the defeat of Nazi Germany, culminating in transporting the men and materials for the D-Day landings.

By 1945, Britain's worn-out railways were in a parlous state. With Labour in control, nationalisation appeared to be the only option and, on 1 January 1948, British Railways was born.

TRAVELLING ON
THE CONTINENT

WYNNE JACKSON + 1910

*The personal diaries of Wynne Jackson reveal
a journey from Britain to the continent*

30th May

IMAGINE IT! Here am I in the Dover Express actually speeding away to Naples to meet Ell who is to arrive there the same day as I on 1st June. An early breakfast and start from Aldershot coming up by the 9.20 with my dearest who came to the 11.0 at Victoria to see me off. It is a glorious day and we are hurrying through Kent with its hop gardens and fields of strawberries and fruit orchards, the country is looking lovely, fields are golden with buttercups and all the may is in full flower. I have a 1st to myself, and as breakfast was at 8.0 have just availed me of my tea basket and made myself some tea which was most acceptable. The excitement of going abroad like this is too wild for words. I have not been out of England since our honeymoon, 9 years ago this June.

Later: the crossing is over … and now it is about 5.30 and we have passed Amiens on the way to Paris. I have just been making more tea with which I regaled a travelling companion and self much to our mutual refreshment. Tea – what an invention it is, it makes a new man of one but the t.c. has a forbidding Mother with her and not being bold enough to ask permission to smoke I took the opportunity of doing so when I went to wash my cups in the lavatory! We get to Paris in about an hour now, and have just passed 'Bass Pale Ale' – how odd! One doesn't see French adverts on our rail sides at home.

Reached Paris and went round in the train to the Gare du Lyon, a most leisurely procession stopping in every siding and all the small stations on route, at length we arrived and I got hold of Cooks man who after I had had dinner put me into the Rome Express.

31st May

Well as I write this we are rushing through the Mont Cenis Tunnel. It takes half an hour and atmosphere is just suffocation. We passed a pretty restless night, the old man (who was sharing the compartment) and I. I say we because the poor one was bungling about so much changing his coat and his seat, moaning and mumping that there wasn't much sleep for me! It is now about 12.0 as I write and we do nothing but rush from one tunnel to another. The country is perfectly superb. It is getting pretty hot and I am longing to get into white clothes but the dirt in the train forbids it. I keep on washing but to no avail, each time one touches anything one's hands are black – as we pass each small station there stands the station 'mistress' holding her trumpet and what looks like a telescope and when we stop anywhere we are not allowed to move until a blast is sounded, making a noise like a peacock. I want to take some photos on the way but I hear they are very averse to cameras in these parts so I have hidden mine for the present ... we have just been to *dejeuner*, a real Italian meal and very good but it wasn't the least pretty to see them shovelling in the *spaghetti au tomates* leaving long strings hanging out of the corners of their mouths!

THE WAR FROM THE TRAIN, PART 1

MAJOR A C CHAUNCY • 1914

Notes and impressions on how the First World War
is affecting the Great Eastern Railway (GER)

STANDING ON THE PLATFORM at Liverpool Street recently, watching the movements of train loads of troops, I found myself chatting with one of the seniors from one of our offices. Owing to the absence on their country's service of so many of the juniors, some of the men left behind were, he said, doing boys' work in the office – just so, and some of the boys are now doing *men's* work at the front and elsewhere. It is a pleasure to see the marked improvement in health and carriage in the troops who come in and out of the station, whether in small detachments, or in train loads. They are different men. This is the effect of living the simple life and doing ten hours' drill a day. Great business was done in tea by our refreshment department with some of the troop trains passing in and out of the station in early October. Passed along the platform and sold from great urns at a penny a cup, it went like hot cakes. I think the soldier of my younger days would have turned up his nose at tea. *Tempora mutantur* – I think for the better.

I have seen a letter from a Great Eastern man, a Territorial, who has been on duty guarding railways etc. He writes: 'I have been doing duty on the GW [Great Western] & L&SW [London and South Western] but I still love the old Eastern. We have a lot of railway chaps in our tent and I am loud in praise of the old GER as one of the best.' What do you think of that, my masters, for *esprit de* 'Company'? Even from the front their hearts go back to us. I read in an epistle from the trenches: 'I shan't be sorry to get back to the old department.'

One of our Liverpool Street ticket collectors happened to be going down the line recently, having a Sunday off. He looked very smart as a corporal of the line. I could see his grin when one of his work-a-day colleagues asked him for his ticket.

It is plagiarising the language of the War Lord to say that one's heart bleeds for anything, but surely many Great Eastern men had a tear for Antwerp in her agony. We who have seen the 8.40 off, many a night, laden with holiday makers going to accept the hospitality of the brave Belgians; we, who have been to Antwerp, were staggered to think of it in flames and ringed about by steel. ...

A friend of mine at Parkeston tells me he has seen not one but many of the poor people who have lost their all in Belgium kneel openly on the quay, immediately on leaving the steamer, and offer up a prayer of thanks before proceeding to the train. ...

The ambulance train which occasionally comes into and out of Liverpool Street on its way 'twixt the North and South of the Thames, with its load of wounded warriors, is a pathetic, but not an unpleasant sight. I hesitated about accepting the first opportunity of going to see it, but I am glad I went. It is interesting to see in what great comfort these poor fellows travelled. They all seemed cheery and hopeful. One of the attendants told me, and I was glad indeed to hear it, that by far the greater number of them would make good recoveries. Modern surgery is indeed a different thing from the old system that one reads about in the stories of battles of the last century ... But the sight of these poor victims of the war brought war very close to our homely Liverpool Street Station.

JOINING
KITCHENER'S ARMY

C J HUTCHERSON • 1914

A member of the Great Eastern Railway Goods
Department describes how he signed up to the war effort

'YOUR KING AND COUNTRY need you!' This appeal,
together with the accounts of German atrocities in Belgium,
could not fail to stimulate all young men to answer the call to
arms, and, as a party of four from the Chief Goods Manager's
Department, we decided to throw in our lot with Lord Kitchener's
army and proceeded to enlist. Upon reaching the recruiting
office the first man we saw was a colleague with similar intentions,
propping up a pillar in the centre of the room. After waiting for
a long time in the crowded entrance hall without visible means
of attaining our ends, we enlivened matters with a little song,
and were severely reprimanded by the hefty commissionaire in
charge. He rebuked us in such a thunderous voice that we
withdrew to the pavement outside to discuss matters and get
over our fright. We decided we hadn't enough pluck to face that
awful frown and voice again, so wended our way to another
recruiting depôt where we were more fortunate, and having
been questioned as to whether we had ever been to prison, and
upon other points usually considered personal in the civilian
world, we were immediately whisked before the doctor, who
certified us as sound.

At 8.45 the following morning we were due to appear before
a commissioner to be sworn in. Here we found many boy scouts
making themselves useful in the recruiting office conveying
messages, etc. One youth, standing 3ft nothing, was told to take
one of the party, who stands over 6ft, to be sworn. In a very stern
voice the lad said: 'What's your name?' The name was duly

communicated, and the boy ordered the lengthy one to proceed into a corridor where there was a row of chairs, and said, 'Sit down!' The recruit tried to protest that he would rather stand, but this was received with contempt, the boy saying in a still sterner voice, 'Sit down when you are told to' and such was the sheer brass of the lad that the long one slowly sank into a chair

crushed. He remarked afterwards that if the boys in the office treated us like that whatever were the regular drill instructors going to be like! – it made us all tremble to think of it.

After being sworn in and receiving the King's shilling, and also 6d. for our fare to — Church, where we were told to report ourselves the following morning, we were now all members of the — Regiment, otherwise known as the 'Steelbacks'. We have not been able yet to fathom the origin of this name, some saying it means that they will never be beaten, and others that they would steal anything, even off one's back. The latter, of course, is a wicked libel from other regiments who are jealous of our splendid record.

Nine o'clock the next day we arrived at — Church and not being sure of immediate marching orders we took our wardrobes in our pockets. After waiting on the tip-toe of expectation for two hours listening to the names of recruits being called we sank into a lethargic condition on the church steps. The hours crept by and a member of the party, suddenly awakening from one of many dozes, broke the monotony of the proceedings by doubling out and answering to a name under the impression it was his own, and upon the error being picturesquely pointed out to him he hastily retired to the main body of the party in confusion. Eventually when our names were called we were like Rip Van Winkle. We were then marched off under a commissionaire to — station where we were placed in the buffet and told to wait his return, as he had to despatch other people to Scotland. This, with reluctance, we did. On his return we noticed he had a great peculiarity, viz., drinking his 'cup of tea' in one operation; he explained that this was because he had once had one knocked over. We duly entrained for — and upon arrival at barracks were instructed to draw blankets, which was done with great difficulty, the efforts of two only meeting with success. The accommodation under cover being somewhat limited the fortunate (?) two slept on the parade ground, the 'unfortunates' stealing a march by gaining permission to go out to an hotel.

Our first army dinner was rather peculiar. They apparently forgot to supply us with knives and forks, and on the old sporting principle – 'A good big 'un always beatin' a good little 'un' – the big men present had the lion's share.

At 4.30 in the afternoon we entrained (about 900 strong) for the seaside, people lining each side of the road from the barracks to the railway station, and cheering vociferously. The camp was reached in the early hours of the following morning when we were served with tea and immediately got down under canvas. Since then we have improved both in health and physique and are quite happy with our new sphere of life.

GOD SAVE THE KING.

A TRIP FROM THE RAILWAY FACTORY

ALFRED WILLIAMS • 1915

*A former factory worker recounts
the annual staff trip to the seaside*

THE YEAR AT THE FACTORY is divided into three general periods: i.e., from Christmas till Easter, Easter till 'Trip' – which is held in July – and Trip till Christmas. There are furthermore the Bank Holidays of Whitsuntide and August, though more than one day's leave is seldom granted in connection with either of them. Sometimes there will be no cessation of labour at all, which gives satisfaction to many workmen, for, notwithstanding the painfulness of the confinement within the dark walls, they are, as a rule, indifferent to holidays. Many hundreds of them would never have one at all if they were not forced to do so by the constitution of the calendar and the natural order of things.

Very little travelling is done by the workmen during the Easter holidays. Most of those who have a couple of square yards of land, a small back-yard, or a box of earth on the window sill, prepare for the task of husbandry – the general talk in spare moments now will be of peas, beans, onions, and potatoes. The longest journeys from home are made by the small boys of the shed, who set out in squads and troops to go bird's-nesting in the hedgerows, or plucking primroses and violets in the woods and copses. Young Jim was very excited when Easter came with the warm, sunny weather; it was pleasant to listen to his childish talk as he told us about the long walks he had taken in search of primroses and violets, going without his dinner and tea in order to collect a posy of the precious flowers. Questioned as to the meaning of Good Friday, he was puzzled for a few moments, and then told us it was because Jesus Christ was born on that day. Though he was mistaken as to the origin and signification of the Festival, there are hundreds of others older than he at the works who would not be able to answer the question correctly.

At Whitsuntide the first outings are generally held. Then many of the workmen – those who can afford it, who have no large gardens to care for, and who are exempt from other business and anxieties – begin to make short week-end trips by the trains. The privilege of a quarter-fare for travel, granted by the railway companies to their employees, is valued and appreciated, and widely patronised. By means of this very many have trips and become acquainted with the world who otherwise would be unable to do so.

When the men come back to work after the Whitsuntide holidays they usually find the official noticeboard in the shed covered with posters containing the preliminary announcements of the annual Trip, and, very soon, on the plates of the forges and walls, and even outside in the town, the words 'Roll on, Trip', or 'Five weeks to Trip', may be seen scrawled in big letters. As the time for the holiday draws near the spirits of the workmen – especially of the younger ones, who have no domestic responsibilities – rise considerably. Whichever way one turns he is greeted with the question – often asked in a jocular sense – 'Wher' gwain Trip?' the reply to which usually is – 'Same old place' or 'Up in the smowk', i.e., to London, or 'Swindon by the Sea'. By the last-named place Weymouth is intended. That is a favourite haunt of the poorer workmen who have large families, and it is especially popular with the day trippers. Every year five or six thousand are conveyed to the Dorsetshire watering-place, the majority of whom return the same evening. Given fine weather an enjoyable day will be spent about the sands and upon the water, but if it happens to rain the outing will prove a wretched fiasco. Sometimes the trippers have left home in fine weather and found a deluge of rain setting in when they arrived at the seaside town. Under such circumstances they were obliged to stay in the trains all day for shelter, or implore the officials to send them home again before the stipulated time.

'Trip Day' is the most important day in the calendar at the railway town. For several months preceding it, fathers and mothers of families, young unmarried men, and juveniles have been saving up for the outing. Whatever new clothes are bought for the summer are usually worn for the first time at 'Trip'; the trade of the town is at its zenith during the week before the holiday. Then the men don their new suits of shoddy, and the pinched or portly dames deck themselves out in all the glory of cheap, 'fashionable' finery. The young girls are radiant with colour – white, red, pink, and blue – and the children come dressed in brand-new garments – all stiff from the warehouse - and equipped with spade and bucket and bags full of thin paper, cut the size of pennies, to throw out of the carriage windows as the train flies along. A general exodus from the town takes place that day and quite twenty-five thousand people will have been hurried off to all parts of the kingdom in the early hours of the morning, before the ordinary traffic begins to get thick on the line. About half the total number return the same night; the others stop away till the expiration of the holiday, which is of eight days' duration.

The privilege of travelling free by the Trip trains is not granted to all workmen, but only to those who are members of the local Railway Institute and Library, and have contributed about six shillings per annum to the general fund. Moreover, no part of the holiday is free, but is counted as lost time. The prompt commencement of work after Trip is, therefore, highly necessary; the great majority of the workmen are reduced to a state of absolute penury. If they have been away and spent all their money – and perhaps incurred debt at home for rent and provisions beforehand in order to enjoy themselves the better on their trip – it will take them a considerable time to get square again; they will scarcely have done this before the Christmas holidays are announced.

At the end of the first week after the Trip holiday there will be no money to draw. When Friday comes round, bringing with it the usual hour for receiving the weekly wages, the men file out of the sheds with long faces. This is generally known at the works as 'The Grand March Past', because the toilers march past the pay-table and receive nothing that day. The living among the poorest of the workmen will be very meagre, and a great many will not have enough to eat until the next Friday comes round, bringing with it the first pay. The local tradesmen and shopkeepers look upon the Trip as a great nuisance because, they say, it takes money away from the town that ought to be spent in their warehouses; they do not take into consideration the fact that the men are confined like prisoners all the rest of the year.

Work in the sheds, for the first day or two after the Trip, goes very hard and painful; everyone is yearning towards the blue sea or the fresh open country, and thinking of friends and kindred left behind. This feeling very soon wears off, however. Long before the week is over the spirit of work will have taken possession of the men; they fall naturally into their places and the Trip becomes a thing of the past – a dream and a memory. Here and there you may see scrawled upon the wall somewhere or other, with a touch of humour, '51 weeks to Trip'; that is usually the last word in connection with it for another year.

THE WAR FROM THE TRAIN, PART 2

MAJOR A C CHAUNCY • 1915

Further notes on the experiences of Great Eastern Railway employees

WE ARE STILL, in our journeys to and from town, asking each other the eternal question 'How long do you think the war is going to last?' Even the most venturesome of us now will not hazard a prophecy, for, though we hear less of 'Tipperary' and things are generally in a more hum-drum state, there is still that general post of troop trains, there are still soldiers crowding the platforms and, alas, that ambulance train with its sad freight is more frequent in its journeyings.

I have noticed, travelling up and down these last few months, what an inroad the French language had made into our solemn suburban trains. It is of course talked by the many Belgian guests we are entertaining in the GER suburbs. The brand of schoolboy French which was until recently the only French I knew has been wonderfully improved of late, and with the kindly help of our visitors I can make myself intelligible (sometimes). I commend this opportunity of picking up French...

The German concentration camp within view of the line at Stratford must bring the war closer home to us. Those whose business takes them walking along the line in the vicinity of the camp should not loiter, nor let their curiosity get the better of them, because they are apt to be shot first and court martialled afterwards.

I cannot visit Harwich and Parkeston at these times without seeing something to admire in our men and ships who rule the waves. What historic names these Harwich ships have to live up to and how well they are doing it. The people are not unnaturally quite proud of them and in the local parliaments you hear them spoken of as 'our' ships.

The Harwich Hotel is doing bravely as a hospital. They spent a cheery time there on Christmas Day. A feature of the evening was a visit from some French matelots, off some French warships temporarily in at Harwich. They were the guests of the evening and everybody was glad to see them. When I was there recently there were several companies of lads in khaki drawn up outside the hotel, waiting their turn to go in and be inoculated before going to the Front. This inoculation seems to be one of the successes of the war, as, however else our troops may be suffering, they are remarkably free from enteric and typhoid.

Nowadays I think it would be impossible to take a journey up and down the Colchester line, without having at least one man in uniform for company. A short time back I travelled back from Colchester, and was the only man in mufti in a first-class compartment. Besides myself there were four military officers and a naval commander. It is quite interesting to study the rank and regimental badges, also the medal ribbons of these people; you can thereby glean a lot of their life's history in silence. I know a good many of the badges and ribbons, but would like to complete my knowledge were a book published by some enterprising author explaining all about them. A few months back a British Officer in uniform was a rare and interesting sight. I could never understand why our officers were so chary of being seen in uniform. In all the Continental towns it seems to me that the going and coming of the uniformed officers lends a touch of interest and colour to the scene and the war will have accomplished something if it teaches our officers that the King's uniform is worth being seen out in.

A Christmas card I received from one of the GER men serving as an officer in one of our active service territorial battalions is very tastefully got up with the regimental crest and motto in gold and is tied outside with a riband of the regimental colours (dark green and black, if the censor will let me say so). The pictures inside are a portrait of Sir John Moore (the regimental hero), and a picture in colours of Crawford's Light Brigade facing about once more to hold back the attack of the enemy during the celebrated retreat from Spain. All our colleagues, if one can judge from the letters to hand, spent as cheery a time as possible under the circumstances, whether in billets, huts, tents, trenches or mud. They all seem to have been impressed with the mud. Writing as I have to for press convenience, early in January, I hope it is not too late to wish them a New Year that will bring them all victory and an early return to England, home and beauty.

WHAT LIFE
MEANS TO ME

A GUARD ✦ 1923

*A Great Eastern Railway guard of 25 years'
experience looks back on his working life*

IT IS TWENTY-FIVE years since I became a guard on the
Great Eastern. I was allowed a month to learn the 'road' and its
signals; then I underwent the sight tests, and the examination in
routine and emergency duties, after which I became duly
qualified to blow the whistle and wave the flag.

It is sometimes forgotten that it is the guard's first duty, as well
as the driver's, to look out for the signals. That is not always
appreciated by people, who think the guard is just a time-table in
coat and buttons.

If anybody thinks that the guard sits in his van enjoying the
scenery, he is greatly mistaken. It is not generally known that
the guard is in control of a brake which will stop the train
independently of the engine-driver. My very first duty on joining
my train is to see that this continuous brake is in proper working
order. I have to test it again at any point where the engine is
changed, or where coaches are put on or taken off. If the driver
should overrun the signals or anything else happen to necessitate
it, the guard's brake comes into play.

That is not all the guard has to see to by any means. There
are a good many finishing touches to be put to the train before
the start. The guard has to see that the coaches are properly
coupled, and the train labelled for its destination, and that he has
the spare couplings and other things required in the event of a
breakaway of a portion of the train. If the train should break in
two, by the way, both portions would stop automatically. Some
people have quite a dread of the train breaking in two and the

first part going on without knowing anything about it. That cannot happen with the continuous brake, for its disconnection would stop the train. Then he has to make provision for any slips—that is to say, for any portion of the train which may be slipped at a station where the train does not ordinarily stop. That is rather a risky business, though it is convenient for those who want to make fast journeys to less important stations. Then, after the guard has seen that the passengers board the train in the proper sections, he is handed a basketful of letters to sort, to be ready to be given out at the different stops, not to speak of miscellaneous parcels, and rolls of newspapers, and passengers' luggage, anything from a bicycle to a poll parrot. He is also the time-keeper of the train. It is his business to see that the train goes off sharp at the booked time. He puts down on a way-bill the times of the running. He has to report all delays, whether time has been lost by the engine or by the signals. The running of a train may be interfered with by such slight things as wind, rain, and greasy rails.

But 'Safety First' is the rule on the line. The guard's first concern is the signals. It is laid down in the general rule book that the first duty of the guard is to see to the safe working of the train, and after that he can see to the parcels. Really, he needs two pairs of eyes, one to sort his letters and so forth, and the other to mark the semaphores. In the London district the sections are so close that the guard needs all his watchfulness for this latter duty alone. No sooner does one signal flash by than he is looking out for the next. If the 'red eye' be disregarded the guard will share the responsibility with the driver. It is not always realised that there is a look-out on the train behind as well as before. In running a train you keep your eye first on the distance signal, which is a cautionary signal. If that is against you the driver reduces the speed, so that by the time he reaches the next signal, if the arm is still at 'Danger,' he will be able to stop sharp. In running a train you always have to think ahead. Every gradient, every curve, every stopping place has to be prepared for.

Such are the ordinary duties of a guard ... a bit in the big machine. But he has other more sociable duties. Among the passengers he represents the railway company on its human side. When the 'happy couple' go off in the train to the accompaniment of cheers and confetti, they probably never think that the guard has a soft spot in his heart for them (though he is useful when they want a compartment to themselves), but he does really rejoice with them that do rejoice, and he is glad to feel that he has got such happiness in his charge for an hour or two. He, too, has had his days of romance, or, rather, he has them yet, though he is a man with three grown-up daughters. Sometimes there are pathetic things happening on the footboard – mothers saying good-bye to their sons, and, like Rachel of old, refusing to be comforted. That happened often during the war, but one sees it happening constantly, with youths going up from the country to London to make their fortunes, or emigrants setting out for their boats, or children being sent to institutions. There are a good many scenes on railway platforms which make a heavy demand on the sympathies of the guard, and call for all his tact if he is to get the grieving mother out of the carriage and get the train off. I show no respect of persons in my duty. The humblest counts one on my train just the same as the highest, and many a time my heart has gone out to the poor mother whose tears were streaming down her cheeks as she waved her good-bye.

The experience of train travelling gets on some people's nerves. They are sure the train will carry them past their destination, or get switched on to another line or something. And while some people make too many inquiries, others do not make inquiries enough. I remember once, just as our train – a fast one – was moving out of the station, a young lady came running down the staircase and made a dash for it. She stumbled between the footboard and the platform. I instantly applied my brake, but mercifully she was not hurt by the stumble, and she clambered in. At the next stop which was a long way on, I went to her carriage to take particulars, because it is an offence to board a moving train, and then I found that, after all, she had got into the wrong train, and had been carried a long way beyond her destination, where we had not stopped!

In twenty-five years as a guard I have seen a good many changes in railway work and in the conditions of railwaymen. But the best of all changes is the reform on the temperance question. There is nothing now like the drinking there used to be years ago. Very many railwaymen, too, as becomes men who have the lives of their fellows in their charge, are deeply religious. There has been some set-back in this respect since the war, but still one does meet, to one's delight, many God-fearing mates. We have had trains on which the engine-driver, the fireman, and the guard have all been men who were serving the Lord. Somehow, those trains seem to run more smoothly than anything that the oil on the axles can account for. We have godly signalmen too. One of the signalmen in charge of that great cabin at Liverpool Street, in control of all those levers, was converted at our railway mission at Stratford. It is a fine thing to have religious men on the railway line.

Some people might think from my narrative that it is a very tame business having charge of a train. Yet there is a sense in which every moment is dramatic. You feel this especially in a long night run, when your train seems to be the only living thing in all the land, like an awful alligator, as someone put it, snorting along in a desperate hurry.

A RAILWAY
FLIGHT OF FANCY

ANONYMOUS ✦ 1923

A contributor to the Furness & West Cumberland Railway
Magazine *imagines a futuristic return to his home town*

LIKE SO MANY OTHERS, I had left Barrow in the gloomy
days of 1923, when the prospects of the town had been
apparently so hopeless. In America I had succeeded in amassing
enough in the course of twenty years to keep myself in moderate
comfort for the rest of my life, and now in 1943 the longing to
re-visit the old country and my native town had proved irresistible,
and after a week in London, I had made arrangements for my
journey to Barrow.

A few questions, and the obliging officials in the very
comfortable LMS hotel had done the rest. 'Go by train,' they
said, 'the aeroplane is no faster, and very dull.'

On the morning of my departure I was handed a card on
which was printed the number of the platform, the time of
departure and arrival of my train. My luggage I did not see
again until I found it in the room of my hotel at Barrow.

A few minutes before the time of departure, I walked on the
platform, and entered the numbered carriage in which, without
difficulty, I found seat No. 214, which had just been allotted to
me. In a small bookshelf just above my head were half a dozen
beautifully illustrated books, dealing with the history of places
through which the train passed. An earphone was suspended on
a hook close by; on the small table in front of me were writing
materials, a small electric indicator showed the names of stopping
places. 'Crewe', 'Grange', 'Ulverston', 'Barrow'; not 'Carnforth,'
thought I, 'whatever has happened?' Presently I became aware
that the landscape was flying past, though nothing beyond a

gentle humming noise indicated that we were being hauled by an electric locomotive at 80 miles an hour.

After a delightful lunch I must have dozed. When I awoke we were flying through a town which I found afterwards was Wigan, where I noticed a magnificent building, and thought it must be a new cathedral. It was the LMS power station, where, with coal from the pithead, electric power is generated for the Lancashire & Cheshire Sections of the line. After what seemed but a few minutes, we drew up smoothly at Grange, the same as ever, except that the station seemed to have grown. How I revelled in that glorious view across the sands once more.

At Ulverston (it being market day) there was the usual collection of farmers on the platform. How little they had changed, though they all looked prosperous and jolly, very largely owing to the convenient rail rates charged for agricultural produce and the splendid service of LMS lorries which served the trains.

'Now for Barrow,' was my next thought; 'What changes have taken place there, I wonder?' Presently a distant view of the docks showed me something. The Cavendish Dock was full of imported timber, and in it were two huge timber ships unloading. At the oil jetties were two 15,000 ton tankers (surely a new channel must have been cut). Further off one could see the towering hull of a Canadian cattle boat, and a forest of masts belonging to motor liners loading rails, and in a siding stood a train load of Irish produce.

Where once stood the Vulcan Works a huge motor factory was in full swing, and not a vacant piece of land on either side of the line could be seen. But what had happened at the Central Station? Six platforms, and facing it, the beautiful LMS hotel, connected to it by a bridge. A fleet of cars under cover awaits the passenger to carry him where he will at absurdly low fares, but the strangest thing of all was the entire absence of dirt. At last the big works had found a method of consuming their own smoke. I have not space to describe the beauties of the town, but it is enough to say that all my dismal foreboding of twenty years before had not materialised. There were some of us who thought then that elimination of competition, and centralisation in railway matters would spell ruin for towns such as Barrow, but a few hours in this prosperous town have shown how false was the prophesy.

THE 1926
GENERAL STRIKE

R W CARR ✦ 1926

*From the journals of a Yorkshire railwayman
who participated in the General Strike*

THE WEEK OF the General Strike in 1926 was favoured with fine weather and I spent a good deal of it playing cricket on the 'Beck Stees' at Sherburn-in-Elmet. The name of 'Beck Stees' was, I presume, connected with the fact that to reach the area it was necessary to negotiate a couple of stiles … I did however, cycle into Leeds on one or two occasions to attend the RCA (Railway Clerks Association) meetings at the YMCA Hall in Albion Place – a room in the premises having been hired for the duration of the strike. …

I was returning from one of these visits on the first day of the strike and came upon a huge crowd of people at the lower end of York Road in the Marsh Lane area. A tramcar was descending the road, driven by a man not in uniform, but wearing an ordinary suit and a bowler hat – obviously a civilian volunteer or a Tramways Inspector or official. The strikers were in ugly mood and although there were a number of Mounted Police riding around, it was clear that there was no intention of letting the tramcar proceed towards the city, for as soon as it reached the milling crowd, a hail of stones shattered the plate glass windows of the top and bottom decks. The driver was the only occupant of the tram and he quickly left under the protection of the Police, amidst shouts and jeers. I learnt later that at a similar demonstration that day in Briggate, the angry crowd rushed a tramcar and in so doing, Harold Dobbie, one of our station clerks, was pushed by the crowd pressure on to the tram's driving platform, where he was arrested by the Police protecting the driver. ...

The Strike came and of the thirty-six or so clerks attached to the Parcel Office, only about four remained at work. These were the 'senior' men of supervisory rank, who considered it not appropriate to strike. The uniformed staff of porters, vanmen and vanlads came out a hundred per cent. ... Strike pay was fixed at 35/- per week per man, nothing extra for families. Since I was on a salary scale (based on my age of twenty years) of 28/- per week, I was in fact 7/- per week better off on account of the strike. The majority of men were, however, at their full pay scale, which was reached in those days at age thirty-one and this was 76/8d. The Strike lasted about eight days and was then called off. ...

I and the rest of the clerical staff received a telegram instructing us to resume duty at the Parcels Office on the following day. I cycled from home at Sherburn-in-Elmet and on arriving at the Parcels Office, found the other clerks standing outside. I learned that they, on reporting for duty, had been informed that they must first sign a form relinquishing their previous rights to permanency of employment. This they refused to do and in consequence were still out on strike.

Only one clerk, Wilf Clark, a young man who married the previous week or so, decided he could not afford to do otherwise and signed the form enabling him to return to work. This condition for reinstatement was apparently universal amongst the Railway Companies, but was denounced by all the Unions concerned and members advised to remain on strike until it was withdrawn and the return to work was unconditional. ...

The same day it was announced that the Railway Companies had given in to this demand and in consequence we all reported for duty the following day. The Inward Office was the size of a large warehouse and was in stinking condition, for in addition to the hundreds of parcels held over from 1st May there were boxes of fish, meat, fruit, cans of milk and Irish cream, which had lain there for nine or ten days. These perishables were loaded out for disposal by the Corporation's Sewage Works at Knostrop Lane.

THE STRIKE:
DOWN AT THE DOCKS

HENRY DUCKWORTH ✦ 1926

From the diary of a student, one of a group who
volunteered to help unload for Southern Railway (SR)
at Dover Docks during the General Strike in 1926

Thursday, 6th May

BIRKIN, OUR CHAUFFEUR, plus a guard for the return journey, was ordered to be round at Great gate with his 100 mph Bentley at four o'clock. A H S and I were two minutes late, but by 5.30 we had all posted in and were starting down Trinity Street ... Birkin had removed his windscreen in case he should have a brickbat thrown at him in the course of his way back through London. ...

Numerous rumours were about as to the strikers' attitude towards us. It was thought that there would be a massed attack on us during the night or an attempt on the part of a single man to get in and cut the cables of the cranes. The cranes were our most vital spot, upon their being all the work of the day: it would be difficult to exaggerate their importance; it would be impossible to cope with luggage or cargo in the hold of the ship without them. There was one 'blackleg' who could work them, Fletcher by name: for this reason he had to be taken special care of. He was a pleasant fellow eager to do well so as to get taken on by the SR when the strike was over. He had been dismissed by the Company, so rumour has it – for being mixed up in a theft which took place in the hold of a ship. The party of blackleg labour was made up of all the riff-raff of the town. ...

Friday, 7th May

Since we had all come down by road there was at our disposal a large number of chauffeurs and their cars, and it seemed a pity not to make use of them. We therefore offered the permanent service of these to the Southern Railway, pleased to be able to repay them in any way for the kindness there were showing us.

A STATION MASTER'S FAMILY

LAWRIE INMAN ✦ 1929–1962

*The son of a signalman remembers his
father's duties at Poppleton Station*

MY FATHER, CHARLES INMAN, was employed at Poppleton Station, as a porter signalman, from 1929 to 1962. He would work shifts with Tom Gall. The cabin was worked in two shifts, 6am to 2pm and 2pm to 10pm. Mr Fred Dale was the station master.

The signalling was by block bell from Skelton Box, for trains towards Harrogate, up as far as Marston Moor station, and vice versa. My father would look for the smoke at Nether Poppleton, or in the other direction, just before the railway bridge at Upper, and then go out to open the gates. You just had to push one gate and all four would close, then he would go to the ticket office and issue tickets to passengers.

There was a passenger train to Harrogate at 7am in the morning. My wife's father, Johnny Hawkes, would go down to the station with his hand cart loaded up with fresh fruit (strawberries, rasps, gooseberries) and veg (lettuce, radish, cauliflowers, cabbage etc.). He also grew forced rhubarb in season, which was grown in a blacked out shed lit only with candles. My father would help to load it into the guard's van along with bicycles and parcels to be sent down the line. Mr Hawkes would go with the train and deliver his goods to a shop in Knaresborough and would come back to Poppleton on the next train, arriving back at 9am. Then his wife would have his 'drinkings' ready as he called it, and he'd sit there and have his drink and his teacake or whatever it was and then he'd get changed into his working togs and out to work.

Also weekdays, a shunting goods train would come out from York and work the line, dropping off wagons of coal which the station master had ordered from the colliery (Frickley Colliery) in various grades. This would need the other gates opening so the engine could shunt it up the ramp over the various bays in the coal yard. Father would have to unload the coal and help to bag it up for someone to collect and deliver by horse and cart. If someone came for a ton of coal, he would have to help load it and take it over the weigh bridge to weigh it off.

Also a cattle truck loaded with Irish cattle would be delivered from time to time and would be unloaded at the loading dock, and farm hands would drive them to local farms who had ordered them from Ireland. Also he would have to load wagon loads of potatoes to be sold as cattle feed. These would be dyed a blue colour as unfit for human consumption.

On the station was a warehouse. This housed sacks which were hired out to farmers to put ten stone of corn in each to send away by rail. (Each sack cost one penny to hire, at a time when there were 240 pennies to the pound.) Father would have to give them a hand to load the full sacks onto wagons, sheeted down to be collected the following day by the goods train. There would be a destination ticket fixed behind a clip on the wagon. It would be taken to a marshalling yard and sorted out.

The station also took in parcels or anything you wanted delivering anywhere. A mechanical horse, a three wheel flat backed petrol driven wagon, would come out and deliver local parcels etc., and take ones for away back to York, to be sorted. ...

Monday was lamping day when father would climb the signals to put a refuelled and trimmed paraffin lamp in the distant signals. One would be three-quarters of a mile away through the railway bridge, and two others near Nether Poppleton crossings, and a fog lamp which was 200 yards down track towards Harrogate which was on a post about 3ft 6in high. If you could not see it lit and a train was approaching, there were two levers in the cabin, one for up line and one for down, which swung a metal bar onto the track, with a fog cap [detonator] fixed to it.

Poppleton Station used to enter the best-kept station competition, and won it several times. The Station Nursery was situated beyond the loading dock and would grow choice plants for the railway, to be used for displays when important people visited anywhere on the LNER.

THE LEADHILLS TRAIN

ANONYMOUS + 1930s

*A young man's poem, written in the local
South Lanarkshire dialect, to his girlfriend after they
travelled on the Elvanfoot to Leadhills branch line*

The wind was cauld, the rain was wet,
But 'ach' that didna' maitter,
We spent a week-end at Leadhills,
We couldna' spent a better.

The local train is such a scream,
It causes mony a laugh,
I'm sure the men that run the train,
Will hae tae staun some chaff.

They'll stop the train at ony place,
They'll stop it on a moor,
In fact they'll stop beneath a tree,
Tae shelter frae a shoor.

And should a sheep get on the track,
They soun the engines whistle,
Slap on the brakes, come tae a stop,
Then the gaurd gets on a bustle.

Doon the steps he slithers,
While the train is gaun,
He runs along the railway track,
Wi' his red flag in his haun.

He reaches that puir sheep,
And ge's it sic a fright,
That macs it run across the field,
Until its oot o' sicht.

At last they reach the terminus,
They ca' it Elvanfoot
The gaurd looks oot the window,
Crying 'A' youse for here come oot.'

So ends a happy journey,
In an interesting train,
Some day we hope if we are spaired,
Tae dae it owre again.

And though we are at hame noo,
Midst the city's mony thrills,
We never will forget the time,
We spent at Lone Laedhills.

A JOB ON
THE ROAD

ANONYMOUS ✦ 1936–1940

*An Assistant District Canvasser for the London
& North Eastern Railway describes his job*

IN MAY, 1936, I embarked on a new phase of railway work
when I became an Assistant District Canvasser and set out in a
small Austin car to cover an agricultural district allocated to me.
My mission was to make contact with the trading public resident
in villages and hamlets far from any station. It sounded an easy

job and a pleasant change of work, with an open air life and a car to tour the countryside – but I was soon disillusioned.

After the first three months or so I can honestly say I thought I was a failure, I did not seem to be making any headway. Then I adopted new tactics and learned that to achieve success it was first necessary to adapt oneself to the standard of the client (by this I mean to be able to talk with the smallholder or the gentleman farmer in his own particular way) and to acquire a knowledge of their favourite holiday or topic, because I found to my cost that direct conversation with the farmer does not pay. 'I had to bait the hook and let them bite it.' Friendship with the traders was the next step, and I followed different methods to achieve this. Sport helped, and I found that I could talk business easier after a game of golf, tennis or billiards, better than actually in the farmer's house or in his fields. Another method I used was to angle for election on as many social club committees as possible. These factors coupled with an all-round knowledge of commercial work helped me to arrive at the ideal stage when the trader had confidence in me (and there is no doubt that confidence is the goal to aim at) and then despite road competition I began to secure business.

Something must be said of the station master and staff at the stations. They act in the capacity of secret agents to the canvassers. Probably through chance conversation they hear of the likely movements of traffic and many times I have had notes pushed into my letter box saying, 'Come and see me quickly.' On one occasion I went to see a station master and he told me he heard that a certain grower had recently planted 300 acres of celery. I visited the farmer and learned that he intended to market the traffic in London and that road rates were considerably less than our own exceptional rates. Realising that if the traffic was sent to London we should lose the business, I ventured to suggest that a more varied distribution might result in his securing better prices. The suggestion was adopted and as a result we handled up to 30 wagons daily over a period of a few months.

A canvasser's lot is a very varied one. Claims have to be settled and declined, bad debts collected. These tasks are not always very pleasant, and do not mix very well with canvassing. Rail-conducted household removals is a traffic which I had quite a lot to do with. It does not take long to acquire the necessary experience to walk into a house and estimate the weight of furniture, etc., to be moved, but care is necessary. I well remember that the first removal inspection I undertook resulted in my estimate being 10 cwt less than the actual weight, but afterwards I found that the client when moving packed 7 cwt of coal and 2 cwt of potatoes in the container, which, of course, had not been taken into account in my estimate. I always stressed the fact that it was possible to insure the furniture at a small premium if despatched by rail, and on many occasions used this argument successfully against road competition.

An 'all-in' farm removal is another job undertaken by canvassers, and I found that estimating the weights of implements and carts, and judging the numbers of cattle wagons and horse boxes required, all added to the interest of the day's work. Livestock sales were regularly attended, and at those functions I first made contact with the auctioneer, who would invariably announce … that I was in attendance. Armed with scales for the charging of livestock and timetables, I found that, apart from quoting charges and arranging services for the animals, I was an enquiry clerk quoting services for the return journey of the buyers. These sale days were hectic because usually a string of lorries were in attendance to pick up the traffic. Attendance at Agricultural Shows was another part of my duties … apart from looking after the show exhibits, useful canvassing work could be performed, as representatives of large firms were present.

The securing of pleasure party travel has of necessity to be incorporated with goods canvassing work. I found the public unwilling to be content with a straightforward journey by rail. They required me to arrange an itinerary covering rail journey, meals and road toursm – in fact, I found it difficult to secure business other than by being an organiser for the party. This traffic developed on extensive lines up to 1939, and now when I have a nightmare it is usually associated with either the memories of a crowd of 500 children I took by rail to King's Cross to show them the sights of London, or the occasion when I addressed a body of about 100 members of a branch of a women's institute in an effort to persuade them to go on a rail outing. How I got all the children home safely and attended to their wants, and how I survived that meeting with the ladies I still fail to understand.

CLEANING THE LOCOMOTIVES

CHARLES DAY · 1940s

*A retired steam locomotive cleaner remembers
the effort required to make the engines shine*

THE CHARGE CLEANER were allotted so many hours a week [per] loco, you were. I think for a Pacific you had twelve hours, so that was split up, you were in gangs of four or five ... and the streamliners, the boilers and the tenders they were cleaned in turps, not paraffin, turps, you got paraffin for the wheels and the tender bottom as we used to call it, but the boiler and the tender sides we did in turps, with a solution that they call 'compo' and it was like ... a white liquid solution, a little bit like wallpaper paste ... and we used to ... splash it all on the tender side like that, then you get this, a very clean cloth, especially if it was this sort of weather and they didn't get very dirty then, you know it didn't get a lot of oil splashing up. We used to wring these cloths out ... and we used to get them, wring it well out and then you could wipe all the tender up and they'd come up, they'd shine up lovely. Now, for the smoke box fronts and this applied to the Pacifics as well, if there was nobody looking, you'd get another clean cloth and you'd go to the axle box lubricator and you'd get a rag full of good oil and you could smother the smoke box with that and then polish it all up and the old chargeman cleaner used to say, 'Yes, you so and so's, you've been in that lubricator, 'cos that smoke box wouldn't look like that.' And it was quite true, we did.

[I] sometimes got a little bit of dermatitis with it, you know, because cleaning the wheels and the inside motion, you know the Pacifics were three cylinders engines so you had to get in the pits and so the middle big ends and the connecting rod inside, that was a rotten job working in the pits because they weren't all that deep so you know, you were sort of cramped up and they weren't all very clean ... I would think [the] majority of us, we were pretty good lads, you know ... if you'd work to do we got stuck in and did it and then if it were winter time you'd go and sit in the cab, especially if the loco was in steam and every now and again [a] bowler hatted running foreman would come round and he'd shout, 'Hey, come on, come on down here, get some work done.' You know, and, but by and large the foremen we had then, they were pretty good.

It was a dirty job, yes, but ... barmen, bar lads, now that wasn't a very nice job – getting in the fire box and especially if they'd just come off the pits and had their fire out. I mean, they wouldn't allow you to do it now, but I've gone in the fire boxes, I didn't do a lot of bar laying, you only did the bar laying at Car Loco if the barman got sick or anything like that. But they wouldn't allow you to go in the fire boxes now. I've gone in when there's been a hundred pound of steam left in the boilers, but I mean it was jolly hot in there, and you see the brick arches in the box, they were ... still hot so you didn't want to get near them.

One particular job ... the breakfast train was always a Doncaster job and say, the 10-6 they'd work it to London, come back with the 4 o 'clock out, which was always classed as the heaviest train of the day out of London, 15, 16 cars, and you had to drop some off at Peterborough for Cleethorpes and the loco would get back into the shed at about half seven at night and then the night cleaners would clean ... it every night ... Cleaned regularly, yes, that's right, and they were the ones that, even in the war, that the company ... liked to see them, you know, the breakfast train especially, because you get a lot of business men from Leeds travelling on the breakfast car train and they would come up to the engine and, 'Thank you very much,' sometimes ... drop me half a crown or give you a *Daily Express* or what have you, you know ... we did very well.

KEEPING CALM AND CARRYING ON

ANONYMOUS ✦ 1940

A London & North Eastern Railway employee describes how various staff members have coped during the Blitz

DURING THE PAST three months incessant air raids on this country have given railwaymen a chance to show their mettle. At one time or another almost every part of the line came under fire, but as summer advanced the enemy began to concentrate his attacks on London. Train services were interrupted and damage done to railway property. The staff of all departments have shown commendable calmness in carrying on their duties and have quickly adapted themselves to changes in the normal working which had to be improvised from day to day.

It is not possible to describe a tithe of the good work which was done by our people. All we can do is to give a few instances which have been brought to our notice.

Goods clerk A J Harvey was roused at 2.50am by the pilot of a British aircraft which had fallen on the line blocking both up and down roads. After attending to the exhausted pilot, Mr Harvey opened up the station premises to make contact with the Control Office, the Aerodrome and the Police. He next visited the scene of the accident to collect further details for the Control and finally motored his station master to the site. Altogether a meritorious piece of work during his time off duty.

Mr A E Lowman is a booking clerk at a London suburban station. Mr Lowman was on duty when he was advised of damage by bombs and a derailment at an adjacent station. Acting on his own initiative he proceeded at once to the latter point accompanied by the station foreman and porter. Fortunately their services as first-aid men were not required, but Mr Lowman then took various steps to meet the situation, such as reporting to the local ARP Control Room and Metropolitan Police, and … joined in the inspection of the track for time bombs.

Firemen Gee and Pavelin went into an Erecting Shop and extinguished an incendiary bomb whilst bombs were falling in the adjacent street and glass from the roof of the Shop.

Mr H C C Brown is a booking clerk at a London suburban station. When three bombs dropped beside the station at 5.50pm the force of the explosion threw him across the booking hall against the wall. Though bruised and suffering from shock, he remained on duty until 1.15am helping to clear up, and was again on duty at 9.00am the following day.

A high sense of duty was displayed by restaurant car lad Eric Avory on a journey from London during a period of intense enemy aerial activity. His calm demeanour through the danger zone helped to allay alarm among the passengers and tea was served in a calm atmosphere.

Mr S G Blackmur is a Passenger Department clerk. He was on duty at a station in the early morning when bombs fell and fires started. He entered the booking office and carried to safety various current books and rendered other assistance under trying conditions, well knowing that the fire made the station a target for further bombs.

All these members of staff have been officially thanked for their excellent service during a period fraught with difficulty and danger. We would like to add our own word of appreciation of the fine spirit which they displayed, but indeed railwaymen of all grades have been anxious to keep traffic moving in spite of every obstacle. After an air raid warning has sounded, it is always reassuring to hear our trains puffing along even if the passengers are being conveyed at the speed of a slow freight train. Great credit is due to the locomotive and operating staff for rising manfully to the occasion. It would also be impossible to speak too highly of the energy and resource shown by the engineering department in coping with repairs to damaged lines and stations. Damage to the track has been put right in a surprisingly short time to the greatest benefit of the travelling public.

If the world had been at peace, the past summer would have been remembered for its long spell of glorious days and serene nights. Possibly the railways might have had a record passenger traffic. Our disappointment at the tragic turn of events is intense, but we can comfort ourselves with the thought that the railways have not been wanting in the country's hour of need.

THE WAR, WINSTON AND ME

WILLIAM (BILL) SQUIBB ✦ 1940s

A signalman on the Great Western Railway (GWR) Cheddar Valley line recalls two particular incidents during the Second World War

THE WAR WAS ON and ... [we] could stand in the garden of the house where we were living and ... see Weston-Super-Mare in the distance ... and I was out in the garden working and suddenly 'Whoomph!', looked across, they was bombing Weston-Super-Mare. Presently a plane left there, and he came towards us and as he came across the moors he was getting lower and lower and lower. And there was some soldiers, on the moor and they had a go at him with anti-aircraft gun. And when he came to Westbury-Sub-Mendip – the village that we lived, the station was called Lodge Hill, they didn't call it Westbury because it would have been conflicting with Westbury in Wiltshire, so they called it Lodge Hill – he crept over the top of the village and crashed in the hill at the back.

I was ... doing a bit of gardening and ... some little while afterwards, I heard my wife calling me, you know. So anyway off I went. And she said, 'There's the Station master from Wookey.' So I said, 'Well, that's nothing to do with me.' So anyway, he was a Welshman, and he was talking so fast that I couldn't understand a word he was saying ... my wife said, 'He wants you to get in the car, and go down the station' ... I gathered from him that there was nobody at the station ... And trains were stopped waiting at Cheddar, trains was waiting at Wells – and there was nobody at the station. So I said, 'Well I'll get on my bike.' So I went ... and sure enough, when I got down there, there wasn't a soul at the station – the signalman had gone and everybody had gone. So I turned round to the Station master from Wookey

– and I said, 'Now look, there's certain rules that I've got to carry out before we can start running trains. Bombs have been dropped, there's a plane crashed up in the hills.' So I said, 'I've got to make sure that it's safe for trains to run.'

So we went through all the rules and regulations that I had to go through. Anyway, I – there was a passenger train waiting at Cheddar, so I got the phone to the signalman at Cheddar; I mean he knew as much about it as I did. So I said, 'Well, okay. We'll start the train running from your end 'cause you've got a passenger train waiting, but,' I said, 'remember to tell him, to come in the section under a caution.'

So anyway comes the train, and he got through. And then we started working the goods that was waiting for at Wells … presently the signalman that … should be on duty came running round the corner. So I said, 'Where have you been?' So of course the Station master started having a go at him. So I said, 'Look, I'll leave you two to sort those things out – I'm going home.' So I went home! Next day … when the signalman came on duty that disappeared, I said, 'Here, where did you get to yesterday then?' 'Well,' he said, 'when that plane came over the top,' he said, 'I took after him … I ran all up through the village, ran up over the hills and … there was the plane crashed in the side of the hill.' He said, 'There was three crew on it and they were all dead.' See, so I said, 'Well … didn't you … think … that you were running out on your job?' I said, 'Signalmen don't run out on their job.' I said, 'Any other member of the staff can run away, but a signalman can't run away.' Anyway, he got a couple of days' suspension for that.

I moved up to Dauntsey in Wiltshire right on the edge of Lyneham aerodrome … the war was still on …[and] every time Winston Churchill went abroad, Winston came down to Dauntsey station and they came down from the … aerodrome to pick him up. And it worked out that every time he came and went I was ... the signalman on duty. And ... all we used to get was a little message over the telephone to say, 'Special train be with you in an hour. VIPs on board.' Or, 'To pick up VIPs.'

But they called me up one evening and said, 'Special train be with you. Leaving Bristol in a few minutes' time. Will be with you in about three quarters of an hour.' Now usually the special trains came from London but on this occasion [it] was coming from Bristol. So at first I thought, 'What ... who's the VIP people coming from Bristol?' Anyway the train duly arrived and he ran into the platform and somebody from the platform staff called me up and said ... 'The VIPs on board, they haven't finished their discussions, not yet.' So I said, 'Well you can tell them from me they're not going to finish their discussions on the main line.' So I said, 'I'll set the road for the train to come back in the siding – you stay on the phone, I'll tell you when it's okay.' So, call him up, I says, 'It's okay you can come back now.' And when a passenger train was going back into a siding, he was five miles an hour – very slow. So I was still intrigued, 'Well who's these VIP people from Bristol?' So I slipped back to the signal box window keeping me eye on it going back. And the dining saloon window was open.

And sat in the coach around the table was Mr Churchill, Mrs Churchill, General Smuts [Prime Minister of the Union of South Africa] and Mrs Smuts and two or three more. And as he slowly went by, I said, 'It's all right for you people in there.' I said, 'You've got plenty of food and no work. I got plenty of work and no food.' But I never said it with any intentions that Winston Churchill should hear it, see? The train got back in the siding, I shut it in, started the main line running again. In walks a very tall waiter with a white cloth over his arm, a tray in his hand. And he put the tray on the table and he said, 'With Mr Churchill's compliments.' Afterwards the waiter came back up in the box to get the tray. 'Oh,' I said, 'Will you do something for me?' And he said, 'What's that?' I said, 'When you get back in the train you thank Mr Churchill very, very much for the supper – and tell him to come back soon.'

LEARNING THE JOB: A WARTIME APPOINTMENT

VIOLET LEE ✦ 1940s

Violet Lee joined the Great Western Railway at the age of 17 as a passenger guard for the duration of the war

DURING THE INTERVIEW, it was made quite clear to me it was a wartime appointment, and when the men returned from the forces, we had to resign. Mr Powell gave me a rule book which I had to carry with me at all times and I was to learn the rules as I would have to pass an examination. An important safety rule was rule 55 – when we stopped for any reason between signal boxes, I had to put the hand-brake on in the guard's van, open the vacuum-brake valve – to stop the train moving off – and had to climb down to the ballast and walk back about five hundred yards, and place three detonators ten yards apart on the line and return to the train, and inform the driver you had carried out rule 55. Rule 55, I get asked – people ask me, 'What's rule 55?' And I say, 'Well, it was carried out with such precision, we had – I can't remember any train smashes!' So if a train was coming up on the wrong line and you'd got – there was trouble – and you'd got three detonators on ... the line – they just [made] this horrific 'BANG, BANG, BANG,' so the train in front would know that there was something wrong. And then you, the guard, would return to the van when it was safe to proceed – the driver would inform me with the engine whistle – I had to go back and take the detonators off the line – that's of course if there wasn't a smash – then back to the train, take off the hand-brake, close the vacuum valve – which told the driver the guard was back in the van and he could move off…

There were no radios or train intercom those days. The Great Western Railway was keen to maintain its boast it was the safest railway in the UK. For my training I was put in charge of a senior link passenger guard. You can imagine what an elderly gent he looked to me, a mere slip of a 17 year old girl. Then to get to the position of senior link passenger guard it would have taken him … 30 years. And to pass examinations he moved up through the links and medical examinations every two years. I often wondered what he thought at all these young ladies coming to work on the railways – there was seven of us. He was a very smart man, his serge railway suit was always well-pressed, his brass buttons were well-polished with Brasso, his boots shone, and all his equipment was immaculate. I can still see him in my mind's eye now, with his very wide grey wax moustache, which seemed to stretch from ear to ear. He taught me the ropes – what signals controlled what points – and you can have a gantry with anything up to ten main signals – caution signals – covering ten sets of tracks. Then the guard was jointly responsible, as the footplate staff, driver and fireman, that they were obeying the correct signal – head out of the window, no computer monitors while I sat in a cosy chair – we had to know the gradients, lengths of station platforms – some country stations would take about five eights, and the train may consist of about eight or ten eights. What is an eight? It was the number of carriage wheels, two bogies of four wheels, and with your signalling you had to advise the driver to move forward using the signal lamp, ensuring the passengers stepped out onto the platform and not onto the track. Some very small halts were usually about the length of two eights. I was given a uniform which consists of a round hat …

with 'Guard' in gold braid across the front. We had the choice of shirts … skirts or trousers, because of climbing up and down engines and guard's vans, a brass button tunic top, and a very large pocket watch with Great Western on its face – it was needed to log the times in the log-book drivers and guards had to carry whilst on duty. You logged the driver's name, any defect you found, prior to the commencing of [the journey] … during the journey, the time you left the station, the times you arrived at the stations, and the times you left…If the train was late, you had to explain in writing, 'five or eight minutes late' and you had to explain to Mr Powell, station master, whilst standing on his mat – not a pleasant experience. They gave me a whistle, which had a very loud shrill, a guard's lamp which was lit by wick and paraffin   ooh they were smelly things, we had to clean our own – you flicked the handle round to change the lenses – it had three glasses, green, red and clear – two flags, one green and one red. I was given a second-hand leather bag. It had two straps stitched on the outside to hold the flags, it also held packets of detonators, road notices (i.e. works taking place on the track), speed restrictions, this had to be checked at the office at the start of duty, and you signed to say you were aware of the notices – no excuses! You also checked with the driver. I always wore white cotton blouses, black flat shoes   the latter was necessary … for climbing up to footplates, guard's vans, walking on ballast, and platforms, a great number of country platforms were made of a slatted wood. And I always felt very smart. Well, I must have been the youngest passenger guard ever, and I loved it.

EVACUATION:
A GUIDE

ANONYMOUS ✦ 1941

The London & Northern Eastern Railway
Magazine's *guide to evacuation procedures*

EVACUATION IS REGARDED as an important measure of civil defence and although much has been written of its problems and difficulties, not enough has been said of the co-operative spirit which exists between those who are in any way connected with the movement of evacuees...

It will perhaps be interesting if some details are given of the present arrangements. The schemes recently operating from London cater for the movement of (*a*) unaccompanied school children and (*b*) mothers and children.

As to the working of the schemes. Bombing on London naturally affects the numbers registering and the special trains to be run depends on this and the billeting areas available.

Let us consider the preliminaries before specials are arranged, for instance, on a Thursday. Registrations at local centres have been proceeding and on the previous Monday details have been furnished to the London County Council who ascertain from the Ministry of Health the reception areas available. On Tuesday the Railway Operating Headquarters are conferred with and times of trains are agreed. It remains then for the LCC [London County Council] to advise all those responsible for moving the evacuees from the assembly points; this entails the provision of police assistance, escorts, station and train marshals, nurses, and, in conjunction with the London Passenger Transport board, the omnibus schedules for picking up the parties. The Ministry of Health notifies the receiving authorities which in turn arrange local transport from the detraining stations.

On Wednesday a medical examination of the children takes place and on our part the special train notices are issued to all concerned, prior advice by telephone or telegraph being given [to] the entraining and detraining stations, also the principal departments affected by the movement.

On Thursday, according to schedule, all is ready for the actual journey; the empty train is at the platform with steam heating functioning so that the compartments are warm and comfortable.

The various sections of the train are indicated on the coaches and the station marshal chalks on the windows the respective party numbers. It is an unfortunate fact that occasionally several of those who have registered do not turn up, which accounts for some compartments remaining empty.

Already buses are unloading mothers, children, prams and an assortment of cases of all descriptions on the pavement at the entrance, and here we must give credit to the London Passenger Transport Board and their bus drivers who commenced picking up parties from the various assembly points (generally schools) as early as 8.30am, often having to find their way to six different places between say, Acton and Dalston, and maintain the schedule laid down for their itinerary.

Loading proceeds smoothly and, unless diversions have upset the running of some of the buses, the train leaves to time at 11am Each child wears a label with name, home address, and party number, and on this are also marked various medical symbols. In one case a label was lost, but the child found another. It is not recorded what the billeting officer said when he read 'When empty return to March!'

Escorts and leaders, who assist generally, accompany the party in the ration of one to fifteen persons, but to prevent accidents the doors of the compartments containing only children are locked.

On the journey medical cards are collected and the train marshal, assisted by the nurse, collate details for the receiving authorities, the nurse also rendering any attention necessary, although this is usually no worse than train sickness or very occasionally some minor injury such as a damaged finger.

At a suitable point en route a pre-arranged halt is made for refreshments (hot milk, tea and buns) provided from our refreshment trolleys and distributed by our escorts. On certain sections, however, where long journeys are involved, restaurant cars are attached and a meal is served en route.

The next stop is for the purpose of detaching a portion for a different route or for setting down some of the parties, the train afterwards proceeding with the remainder to the ultimate destination.

At the detraining points the billeting officers, other officials and helpers meet the train and the necessary transport is waiting, telegrams having been received advising details of the parties, prams, etc., travelling. The next move is to a distributing point, again generally a school, where a light meal is served and any necessary medical examination carried out. The writer on one occasion was invited to accompany the party and in conversation with the County Medical Officer of Health mentioned how bonny looked the local school girls who were acting as waitresses. 'Local be hanged,' was the reply, 'they are your London girls who came down in September, 1939, and they don't want to go back either!'

Now for the final move; buses draw in and pick up parties for the various villages where billets are waiting, the marshal and escorts carry on to assist in smoothing out any difficulties such as that of the mother with five children who are anxious not to be separated and so on.

Here we must leave the evacuees in good hands, recalling in our minds those words of [John] Masefield:

'And he who gives a child a treat
Makes joy bells ring in Heaven's Street
And he who gives a child a home
Builds Palaces in Kingdom Come.'

THE WATCH
ON THE LINE

ANONYMOUS ✦ 1941

A London Company Commander describes the contribution
of the London & North Eastern Railway (LNER) to the war effort

THE WAR OFFICE sanctioned the formation of a London
(LNER) Battalion Local Defence Volunteer [LDV, later to
become the Home Guard] Corps early in June 1940. It was on
17th June 1940, that three Group Organisers were selected to
operate in the London area under the guidance of the
Commanding Officer, Captain E F Warren. At a Conference
held that morning these officers were instructed to formulate
schemes at all Stations and Depots of the LNER in the
Metropolitan Police District, and to mount guards and sentries
at the earliest possible moment. Many applications had been
received from members of staff offering their services as
parashots [a term used to describe the volunteers who might one
day shoot invading paratroopers] in the LDV unit. Emerging
from the Battalion Orderly Room, arms filled with a mass of
white forms, Army forms, LDV Identification Cards and home-
made armlets, the task of contacting individuals, completing
attestations and placing men on guard and sentry duty appeared
only a remote possibility. However, guards were mounted that
night, and it is with gratitude that we remember those of our
colleagues who from office, shop, station or footplate paraded

under patrol leaders at dusk. Those stout fellows, whose signature on their enrolment forms had scarcely dried, turned out armed with such weapons as golf clubs, shunting poles, pickaxe handles and police truncheons to patrol the track, act as sentries at vulnerable points, keep a watchful eye for saboteur or parachute invader, and otherwise undertake until dawn the defence of railway property.

The writer has just spent the three nights of Christmas Eve, Christmas Day and Boxing Day on visiting rounds, escorted by the Company Sergeant-Major, to the formations in an East London area. The alert sentries, now warmly clad in battledress and greatcoats, and equipped with the usual impedimenta of the modern infantryman, challenge intruders from their point of vantage in a most businesslike manner, and leave no doubt in one's mind of their ability to use their loaded weapons.

A visit of the Guard Room follows, and here, thanks to the generosity of the LNER and the Territorial Army Association, waiting rooms and other premises have been converted into comfortable rest rooms for the Guard 'off duty', and recruits and others undergoing instruction. There is a warm and friendly atmosphere, but withal an air of readiness to turn out, whether it be to render first aid to casualties, search the track and railway premises for unexploded bombs, extinguish incendiary bombs, or to verify the *bona fides* of a subject.

In the short six months since its inception, a great transformation has take place. Eight companies have been formed covering the whole of the LNER territory in the Metropolitan Police area. The selection and appointment of Officers and NCOs [non-commissioned officers] has been followed by the issue of arms and ammunition (including automatic weapons), an early supply of denim overalls, followed in the late summer by warm battledress and later greatcoats.

The equipping of the first four thousand with boots, anklets, battledress, greatcoats, belts, haversacks, caps, eye shields and even anti-gas ointment, has been smoothly carried out. This task, and the important training programme embracing drill movements, march discipline, rifle exercises, musketry, including the care and cleaning of arms and instruction in the use of automatic weapons, bayonet fighting, fieldworks, map-reading, anti-gas, signalling and fieldcraft and elementary tactics, and physical training, has only been made possible by the keen enthusiasm of all ranks, who, in spite of their ordinary jobs in an essential and reserved occupation, have devoted so much of their leisure to imparting and receiving instruction in military matters.

So advanced had become the training of this formation that within three months of the first enrolment the Battalion had the honour of being inspected by Brigadier-General J Whitehead, CB, CMG, CBE, DSO, the Area Commander, at Loughton Sports Ground. Since that date even greater strides have been made, and the personnel has received its baptism of the intensified night bombing of London. In this connection, no praise can be too great for the meritorious acts performed by all ranks who, fearless of the consequences, have 'carried on' when various stations, including London termini, have been attacked, and at suburban stations when they have been bombed from their guard-room premises. Much assistance has been rendered to the local services in dealing with outbreaks of fire on property adjacent to the railway track, too.

We deeply deplore the losses in our ranks due to enemy action, and, in order to maintain our proud record of increasing numbers of guard duties performed since the Blitzkrieg, shall be glad to enrol on our strength any member of the staff who has not yet been able to give his services.

MANNING THE SWITCHBOARD

BETTY CHALMERS ✦ 1942

*Betty Chalmers worked on the teleprinters and switchboard
at York Station during the Second World War*

WE WERE ON the station [at York] ... fortunately I wasn't on
duty, but there were some, there was one girl on duty and three
men and apparently the bomb hit the station. They'd already
put a thick concrete thing on our glass roof, which was stupid
of course, but they thought it was to save us, keep the light out
as well. Two o'clock in the morning of course, they hit the
station, because that was an important thing to do, and to my
knowledge it's the only time that York station was closed for
two days while they cleared the rubbish because it was terrible.
So I cycled into work next morning dodging broken glass and
carrying my bicycle, got to work, no office, completely destroyed.
But they had taken the precaution earlier, two or three years
earlier, of putting a duplicate switchboard in the shelter under
the bar walls...

 That's partly why we had to work nights ... on the switchboard.
So that was a Godsend because the other one was completely
destroyed. And when I got to the office, well, when I got to the
station amid the rubble, the boss was there and the girls were
sorting out wet railway tickets. The water had come in over the
booking office, and of course, there was nothing for us to do,
nothing, and my mother was ill so he said, 'Well, I think you'd
better go home for a day or two,' which I did ... And the board
was kept going and they hastily got teleprinters from such places
as West Hartlepool and Middlesbrough ... places that weren't as
busy as us, and they managed to put them in the shelter. We were
in a corridor [under the wall] ... it was awful, and they were

there for nearly two years until they cleared some of the muniment rooms in the new offices ... the air conditioning was rough, so in the middle of winter you sort of, when you got there, got down to your bikini nearly, not quite in those days, but nevertheless it was happy. The control were in there, they made a lot of fuss of us girls and ... there was a central control and a district control, the central control was obviously the main one, the district would be this area, the north-eastern area. Yes and the District Intelligence they were down there, so we just had to be in the corridor ... they were very good because we were on our own, they'd say, well you know, 'Do you want something to eat?' And we had a little kitchen and they would give us something or make us something, or the messenger would go over to the canteen if we wanted it and brought it over ... it was terrible. No windows ... and it was hot, it was, when you went in on a winter's morning about six o'clock, oh. You were so cold cycling down, but you know you got used to it...

[there was no loo there] Ah, well now this was tricky, because we had to go, we had to go through the central control, and as you went through they held their hand out for a penny! And we were only quite young but we just had to put up with it, that was all, and in those days, of course, things were, you weren't so free with people ... And then ... I was working in the office normally, but it was my turn on the switchboard and there was a group of Royal Engineers stationed in York. They had come back from France and they were a railway construction company, and some of them started ringing up the girls, realising there were girls on the switchboard, and I know a few of my friends did, and I used to say, 'No, I'm not doing a thing like that.' However, one night this Scotsman came on and he said, 'I'm a Scotsman from Wales.' I married that man three years later!

THE BIG FREEZE

BRIAN PALFREYMAN + 1947

*A retired railway worker remembers his time
as a locomotive fireman in Derbyshire*

THE BIG FREEZE UP ... on the Ashbourne line ... We'd two snow plough engines, they got fast in, there was a 29 foot drift into the Hindlow Tunnel them days, it had built up and they was trying to [clear it] with a snow plough and it packed ... that hard, they couldn't do anything at all ... there was a train coming from Port Sunlight with 500 soldiers to help to dig ... the drifts out.

Anyway this train, he'd come with a Midland Number Four, 0-6-0, and he'd ten coaches on and he'd come from Stockport up the banks on his own, and when I got on the engine, we always used to look at the fire to see what condition it was in and it was blue, which was a very bad sight, it was a dirty fire. So they sent a little Midland Number Three to assist us up to Hindlow, where the drift weather, the snow, was blocking the line and we had to stop for a blow up half way up, up the bank towards Hindlow ... And we got up there and there was Derby inspectors there and a lot of officials and ... they got mattocks, shovels, picks, they'd got all sorts in the guard's van each end and when the soldiers, they'd been in a hot train from Port Sunlight, with the steam heating on and they was fainting, they was going over with the cold a lot of them, you know, they just couldn't stand it. So the chap in charge from Derby he said, 'Oh, get them all on board, back,' he says, 'We've got two jet engines coming tomorrow, we'll shift it tomorrow with these jet engines on low wagons.'

It was an aeroplane engine, the very early jet engines, you know, and they were strapped to this special wagon and they come the next day, 'cos we took them back, all the soldiers back to Buxton that day. And the next day they come and it was just like a candle where the drifts, he'd shifted nothing because it was fast you see. Going up where it was, through the fields where it wasn't so bad then, it could shift it, but ... they had to leave that line until it thawed out on its own. And as I say, it snowed ... every day in Buxton and believe me it was coming crossways, not down, the wind and the freezing wind was terrible. And as I say, it blocked up, probably the end of February because we ... kept sending snow plough engines to try and keep it but it got the better of them and it didn't open until June.

THE CIRCUS COMES TO CAMBRIDGE

SIDNEY SHELDRICK ✦ LATE 1940s

A goods guard in the Cambridge area remembers the arrival of the Bertram Mills Circus train

BERTRAM MILLS COME into Cambridge, and they all come in our extra duties and I used to be the foreman ... We used to be allowed 24 hours, on duty for the Bertram Mills Circus, and we used to be there six o'clock at night on the Saturday night and your first train was due in at midnight. My District Inspector ... they'd meet us in our office, and they'd explain the four trains to you ... the first thing you had come was the king pins ... the big poles which erect your tent, there was always them come in advance to them first and they was always the first to go away to the next place ... which they used to go down to Ipswich from Cambridge. And the District Inspector, he'd explain all these trains because when you got these in the coal field in the dip – that's where we used to unload them ...

they had what they call bow bells – ten of those … which has got all the big stuff on – big vans and things like that, they used to let them in first … and then of course the next thing you got was like all your conflats [term for a flat container wagon] and that with your circus caravans and all that … to come up and one at a time you had to unload all those see, so that was the next job.

[The circus workers] they'd come up on the first train. And their coach used to be on the front … a fella called Basil, he was the Bertram Mills foreman and it was the biggest pantomime in the world … [the train] used to be full of people, and out these circus fellas get with just their vests on scratching their heads, swearing and cursing like you know, because Basil had woken them up. So that was the first pantomime. And we used to walk away in disgust, wouldn't say nothing you know – we'd leave them to it! So these were the people … and they only used to sleep on bare boards, there weren't no mattresses or anything like, you know. And the fella who was with the elephants – he used to live with the elephants, he used to sleep in the stall with them … Anyway, we used to put the animals down in number … three platform, which if you had a camel, which was one funny experience. A camel – they used to have a horse box which was an ordinary horse box and it was an SCB which is a bit bigger one, you know what they put two or three horses in together. And … we used to have … a bit of a pantomime lad … on the station, and we were round there one morning just getting the camels – the man was just getting the camels out, on the Sunday morning, and … on the humps they lay – hung down the side see, and old Bud said to him, 'How do you get them … camels out that truck like that see?' He said, 'Well we let the wind out of the humps!' You know – that tickled him to death see.

Now the last thing in there used to be the elephants, which they were always the last to go down because they used to have a parade from Cambridge like you know, down to the circus, which all the children used to enjoy. But one pantomime was we used to have a foreman, and he used to be full of fun and he come round number three and they – there were bowls contests down number three platform with elephant dung, you know. Bowl them as far as you could and old Carrington [the foreman] used to have tears coming out of his eyes.

END OF AN ERA

1948–1968

By 1948, Britain was in debt following the war and the newly formed British Railways faced an uphill struggle to rebuild and modernise its 20,000 route miles. A crumbling infrastructure, left over from the Victorian age, used mainly worn-out steam locomotives and rolling stock and suffered from outdated working practices, overmanning, union disputes and strikes. As the losses to the public purse mounted and increasing amounts of freight and passenger traffic went to more competitive road transport, it became clear that something radical was needed.

Pruning loss-making branch lines was overseen by the Branch Lines Committee, and around 3,000 route miles were closed between 1949 and 1962. During this period, the railways lost out further to road transport following damaging national rail strikes.

British Railways continued to build steam locomotives between 1948 and 1960, with around 1,500 tried-and-tested locomotives from the Big Four being produced along with 999 of its own standard designs. New all-steel passenger coaches and goods wagons replaced pre-war wooden vehicles. The publication of a 15-year Modernisation Plan in 1955 was a worthy attempt to drag the railways into the modern age but aspects of it, such as hurriedly introducing untried and unreliable diesels, left much to be desired. The plan was stopped in its tracks by the infamous 'Beeching Report' of 1963, following which around 4,500 route miles and 2,500 stations were closed and over 65,000 jobs lost.

The eradication of steam haulage on British Railways in August 1968 marked the end of a 150-year era during which Britain had led the world. Britain's railways had finally reached rock bottom.

THE TRAIN
SPOTTER

STAN KNOWLES + 1940s–1950s

*A rail enthusiast talks about his childhood train spotting
experiences in and around Poppleton Station*

FOR SEVERAL YEARS a lot of children from Upper and
Nether Poppleton spent a lot of time train spotting. It was a train
spotter's Utopia with the Poppleton branch line and the London
North Eastern Railway main line from York to Edinburgh.
There were six points that we used to go train spotting.

On the Poppleton line it was at the old railway bridge and
Poppleton Station. When we went train spotting on the main
line, we would sit on the Churchyard wall at Nether Poppleton,
or we would go down across the fields opposite the Council
houses in Sandy Lane or we'd go further along down what we
called 'Tin Pan Lane'. It was a lane that ran from just immediately
this side of Nether Poppy level crossing, down to the main line.
There was a bridge where you could go – under the main
line. This lane then ran right up the other side of the line, on the
River side of the line, it terminated in a gate into a field and we'd
go through that gate and climb up to where there used to be a
water tower. By this time, we're getting fairly near the Water
Works. At this time Skelton North Marshalling Yard was in full
use and apart from the main line traffic there was a great deal of
goods activity and shunting taking place.

So, to return to Poppleton Station, at that time there were six
crossing gates, six separate gates. Those straddling the York to
Harrogate line were all interlinked and the crossing keeper
would just push on one gate and all the others would open and
shut in unison and as they came to fully open, some limit stops
would come up out of the road and they would be locked in that

position. These were manually operated, but they were all inter-linked by a system of levers that actually ran underneath the road. To give access to all this leverage, the roadway crossing was then wood … there was a set of points round – about where the cattle dock is. The cattle dock's still there now … there was a short siding which came across the road and that had its own two crossing gates and once over the road the track rose quite steeply up and over the coal cells, I think there were either three or four coal cells. There were a lot of goods trains then that stopped at every station en route from York to Harrogate, both picking up empty wagons and leaving wagons with coal and other goods, steam locomotives would push the coal wagons up this steep rise up and over the coal cells and then they would be left there for the crossing gate keeper to release the doors underneath and drop the coal down into these cells…

At the side of this line where it rose steeply, there used to be a weigh house and at the side of the weigh house, just through the gateway that's still there into the coal cell yard, there was a weighbridge, this access was also access into Hutchinson's field which is at the back of this.

The first recollection, this is before I had any real interest, this is a time when I was going with my Mother when she was helping the various farmers during the War years, seeing locomotives – they must have been quite old locomotives, because they had very tall chimneys, possibly three foot in height and these huge domes in the middle of the boiler, which was the regulator housing and steam collecting area. But coming to the locomotives that were in use when I became interested, the majority of the passenger traffic was hauled by the Gresley-designed Hunt and Shire class. Now I can remember several of the 'Hunt' names, there was the 'York and Ainsty', the 'Bramham Moors', the 'Morpeth' and the 'Fitzwilliam' – those were just a few of the names of the engines that ran. They were 4–4–0 wheel arrangements and as I say there were some 'Shires', I think there was one 'Yorkshire' that sticks in my mind, I can't name any others specifically, at the time it was quite something.

We used to make a point of going down to the station to watch the six o'clock train to see it, get its number, and see what it was. When you looked up to the railway bridge, the old railway bridge, the line was on a slight curve as it came under the tunnel. On some weekends when the main line was closed, all the main line expresses – especially those heading south – would come through Poppleton and I've seen all what you might call the 'crack' express types actually come through Poppleton. The A4 Pacifics, the A3 Pacifics like 'The Flying Scotsman', V2s and several other types. It used to be a lovely sight when they were pulling a full rake of newly-outshopped teak bodied coaches. They really did look beautiful.

Coming back to this occasion, when you looked from the station platform up towards the railway bridge, if it were a streamlined A4 Pacific you could tell straightaway by the frontage of it, but if it was a locomotive with what they called smoke-deflectors on, you could just momentarily see between the smoke box side and the smoke-deflector and it was common place for such engines to come on the Sunday main line expresses, which reminds me – we'd gone up there on a weekday evening to see what was on the six o'clock train – looking up towards the railway bridge I could see what was almost unbelievable, it appeared that this normal mundane stopping train was being pulled by something that had smoke-deflectors on – we used to call them 'winnies'. We couldn't believe this, but sure enough as it came nearer the station there was a main line Pacific on a stopping train at Poppleton; to us as kids this was really something. Now the engine in question was No. 60524, 'Herringbone' its name – we found out later as my interests sort of got deeper and I looked more into things, that it was the last of the Pacifics built under the then LNER Chief Mechanical Engineer, Edward Thompson. As I say, it was quite something ... news got around like wildfire, so for the next week there was a large turn out to see this main line Pacific on a normal stopping train. But eventually it stopped coming and we never knew why, but then, we never knew why it ever appeared in the first place.

THE WORLD'S FIRST HERITAGE RAILWAY

TOM ROLT ✦ 1950

This open letter, printed in the Birmingham Post,
*led directly to the preservation of the Talyllyn Railway
and the creation of a movement that flourishes today*

DEAR —

As you are no doubt aware, the Tal-y-Llyn Railway is the last surviving independent Statutory Railway Company in Britain. It is also the last of the once numerous independent Welsh narrow gauge lines still carrying passenger traffic. Built in 1865 and retaining its original locomotives and rolling stock, the railway is of great historical interest, is within measurable distance of achieving its centenary and traverses some of the finest scenery in Wales.

Owing to the recent death of the owner and Manager of the railway, Sir Hayden Jones, it is extremely unlikely that the railway will re-open for traffic in 1951 unless some practical and financial help is forthcoming. This despite the fact that its popularity with holiday makers is such that demand frequently exceeds present carrying capacity.

It is felt that all who are any way interested in railways will endorse the view that it would be deplorable if the year 1951 should be marked by the permanent closure of this unique and historic railway. For this reason a meeting has been arranged at which it is hoped to found an organised body which will ensure that the railway shall continue as a going concern. This meeting will be held at the Imperial Hotel, Temple Street, Birmingham at 7.00pm on Wednesday 11th October, 1950. The organisers cordially invite you to this meeting and hope you will make every effort to attend.

Lady Haydn Jones has graciously expressed her willingness to consider any practical proposals which may be put forward at this meeting, and it is hoped that her legal representative will be present.

Yours truly
L F C Rolt

A Railway Worker Remembers

John Woodall + 1955

*Several tales from in and around
the York to Harrogate line*

THE STATION [AT CATTAL] was quite large for a country station, it had a cattle dock, parcels shed, goods shed, lamp shed, coal sidings, weighbridge and sidings behind the Victoria Inn to store wagons. Adjoining the station master's house was a cottage which was occupied by a lengthman and his wife.

I was always amazed at the ability to be able to move fully loaded wagons by hand. The secret was a lever, called a pinch bar, about six feet long ... the tapered end was inserted between the line and the wheel and the levering action soon had the wagon moving quite easily, which even I could manage.

When the cattle arrived, usually from Ireland, they would be off-loaded and herded down the roads to different farms. The cattle that were to be herded across the crossing were reluctant to do so, which resulted in them being hit with a stick until they moved.

The coal business was one of the station masters 'perks' and the porter-signalmen were expected to help with the filling and weighing of the coal sacks, for which they were paid a few pence per bag. On occasions I also helped during my lunchtime. The coal sacks were loaded onto the railway delivery lorry, which came on Monday, Wednesday and Friday. ...

E R Johnson, Tree Nurseries, used to send most of their trees by rail at that time. The trees used to arrive wrapped tightly in straw and each had to be individually weighed and despatched on the 4.00pm train. Mr E R Johnson was extremely well dressed with his tweed suit and plus fours and arrived by bicycle to pay his bills promptly. ...

During springtime railway shift workers were in great demand as casual labourers on farms singling sugar beet. They were mostly tired by the time they came to work for the afternoon shift and used to easily doze off to sleep in that south facing signal box. The bells of the block system were of differing shapes, one being round and the other pear shaped, so that they gave a different tone when rung. One of the tricks was to put a matchstick across the front of each clapper, so that if they were dozing or down the platform and heard the bell, not knowing which, the matchstick that had moved was the bell to respond to. When the bells were serviced by the engineer, removing the wooden cover usually revealed a number of used matchsticks.

During the autumn, wagons were provided for local farmers to deliver their sugar beet into and they would be removed the following morning by the pick-up and delivered to the York Sugar factory on a ticket system.

One of my weekly jobs was to cycle to Whixley Post Office, to buy National Insurance stamps, which had to be stuck on to the workmen's cards and were subject to inspection. Anyone familiar with the area would know of the steep hill into Whixley and a steep hill back and this journey had to be done whatever the weather. ...

The station was always well planted with summer flowering plants and the staff took a pride in the appearance. Before the annual inspection for the Best Kept Station, the white line at the platform edge was repainted. On the day of the inspection, a single antique Director's carriage with observation windows arrived at the station for the walk-about. The carriage was pulled by a Hunt Class locomotive and both were in immaculate condition. The carriage had cooking facilities and was provided with a chef.

In the autumn, cuttings were taken from the geraniums to be rooted and overwintered in the office. The bay window of the office was completely filled with tailor-made boxes of rooted geraniums, where they survived in spite of having a poor light source due to the platform canopy. ...

The railway company hired out grain sacks at 1 ¼d. per week or part thereof and each sack had to be followed by the relevant paperwork to enable the hire charge to be transferred to the destination and client, until the sacks were returned. A lot of grain was sent to distilleries in Scotland. Any damaged sacks – usually rodent damage – were repaired in a workshop in Toft Green in York. ...

One Wednesday afternoon, the station master's day off, the signalman Bill Kemp came into the office, to discuss the request from a lorry driver from the York firm of Glossop's who had asked if he could off-load a tandem roller on the parcels ramp. A tandem roller is a ride-on with close coupled rollers that can increase its deadweight by a factor of three by vibrating. This would put the roller on to the platform and Bill figured that if he partly opened the road gates there would be sufficient space to drive the roller through the gates. We couldn't foresee any problems so permission was given. Unfortunately as the driver reversed the roller down the parcels ramp and on to the station platform, the driver panicked and jumped off the roller whilst it was still reversing and it ended on its side on the down line. Bill immediately ran to the signal box and pressed the bell once to alert Kirk Hammerton station and then pressed six times to pass the message 'Obstruction Danger'. Railwaymen will know that the 'Obstruction Danger' signal is sent without the normal preceding 'call attention' bell signal. The signalman at Kirk Hammerton immediately telephoned the signal box to enquire what was going on. The lengthmen were working (foreman Bill Bettley) near Kirk Hammerton and they were requested to return immediately on the workmen's trolley to inspect the damage, if any, to the railway line. Glossop's also arranged with Elliott's of Wetherby Road, York, to send out their five ton crane to lift the roller from off the line. Fortunately there was no damage to the line, but the early evening train from York to Harrogate was delayed and I was able to catch the 4.00pm train home on time.

Station master Ferguson took the above events coolly and sent in his report to say that we were just trying to be helpful to a customer of the railways and no more was heard of it.

One morning there was a broken-down train at Kirk Hammerton and this held up at Cattal the following railway bosses' train (timed to allow senior managers to arrive from Harrogate to York in time for work). This train was allowed to pull into the station whilst the obstruction was removed. The station master put on his hat and strolled up the platform answering questions from the bowler-hatted brigade who couldn't believe that their train was being delayed.

Another time I was working in the office and commented on the speed of a light engine going past. (A light engine is one on its own without carriages or trucks.) The next thing we heard was that the gates weren't closed to road traffic at Kirk Hammerton and the engine had smashed through the gates, fortunately without injury to any members of the public.

One thing that Mr Ferguson and myself had in common was that we were both interested in boats. At that time I had built a canoe and expressed a desire to go to the Norfolk Broads. Mr Ferguson got the railway manuals out and discovered that I could take my canoe as Excess Baggage and with my annual free pass I was able to go to the Broads very cheaply. The canoe cost about 21 shillings for the return journey which made for a cheap holiday.

When the Marston workmen's trolley used to return to Marston the illegal procedure was for the trolley to pass the 'Home' signal which was set against traffic (this was a dismissal offence) and proceed towards the station gates. The signalman then changed the points to allow the trolley to cross over to the down line, to where they turned the trolley towards the trolley hut. This whole procedure made it easier for the signalman who did not have to shut the road gates. One evening when the trolley was returning from Kirk Hammerton to Marston, an Inspector asked for a lift. As the trolley approached the Home signal which was against them, the driver rightly refused to pass the signal and sounded his Klaxon horn; on hearing this the signalmen came out of his signal box waving furiously at the trolley driver for not passing the red signal as usual. The Klaxon was sounded again and the signalman, who I will call Dennis, had to go through the proper procedure of closing the road gates and pulling the signal off.

One tale Dennis did tell me was that one Saturday afternoon, during the quiet period, he left the signal box to go shooting in nearby fields, where he had permission to shoot. He heard a train blow its whistle and looked across to the railway lines to see a train waiting to proceed. It was a seaside special which he had forgotten about. Putting his gun down by the hedge he went over and let the train through. 'How are you going to get out of this one?' asked the station master. Dennis remembered that a steam train had set fire to the railway banking sometime that previous week. A letter was sent to Head Office stating that Dennis had gone to investigate the 'fire' to see if there was any danger to rail traffic. The return letter commended Dennis for his actions.

A LITTLE RAILWAY KNOWLEDGE GOES A LONG WAY

RON WHITE ✦ 1950s

A train spotter attends a job
interview in London

IT HAD ALL BEEN much more difficult than I had expected, right from the moment when my father tipped me out of bed at 06.00 on a Saturday morning and said, 'Go to London and get this job.' A job? I had heard of work but knew nothing of it, having just completed a year in the sixth form without much effort, and been told that I was definitely NOT for an academic career, or anything within the Civil Service (then the only two possibilities for the sons of gentlefolk, which I wasn't). Dad was a Green Line Coach conductor (Route 703, Amersham to Wrotham) and a passenger had left a copy of the *Evening News* on a seat; with an empty coach on the last trip Dad had nothing to do and so, read it, even unto the advertisements. Clearly deciding I would be a dead loss after another year at Challoner's School, he had ringed round one advert offering a job at £104 per annum with the impressively named Ocean Accident & Guarantee Corporation Limited, in Moorgate (all this I absorbed after washing, shaving, breakfast and cycling a mile to the station to catch the 07.29 workmen's train to the City, arriving there long before the staff arrived).

Brandishing the paper, I approached the first person I saw, and told my tale getting the off-putting reply, 'Have we come down to this?' He then directed me to the holy of holies, the first floor suite of panelled rooms where top managers lived, and, eventually, the Company Secretary was made aware of my twitching presence. He admitted that a job existed, what were my academic achievements, if any? I produced my Oxford School Certificate, passes/credits in eight subjects, and he held it cautiously, finger and thumb, by one corner, saying 'never seen one of these, always London, nothing provincial' and with that opened a drawer and extracted THREE papers in Maths, English and General Knowledge and told me to answer them and see him again at 11.00.

I am sure he had decided I was useless but to his courteously concealed surprise I produced enough right answers to compel him to continue. Hobbies? Cricket/football/tennis, good. Philately, excellent. Singing, fine, fine, Brownie points everywhere – anything else? And then, I revealed my interest in railways – the bushy eyebrows shot up, the eyeballs revolved slowly in their sockets, the jowls trembled, speech was withheld but was patently on the way. When it came, I thought, 'Bim goes my two quid a week' for he used the pejorative words, 'You're not a train spotter are you?' Hasty thought – 'Oh no Sir, I'm much more involved than that', waffling about the scientific side of locomotive performance, of track engineering, convincing him I might pop round to the Institute of Mechanical Engineering if I was unworthy of his attention (for two quid a week!). He sighed deeply, saying, almost to himself, 'We've never had a train spotter on the staff, can't start now' and then he turned and said 'Is there anything you can do to help and avoid the stigma of being one?' And then, my two quid was saved by the magic words 'ferro-equinologist, student of the iron horse, sir'. He beamed, honour was satisfied, I got the job (the only one I ever had) and we all lived happily ever after.

Working as a Guard in Scotland

Mohammed Ayub + 1950s

Born in Kashmir in 1930, Mohammed Ayub worked as a passenger guard at Stirling

BEFORE I WENT to Stirling, one of the drivers at Thornton Junction said to me, 'There is a foreman at Stirling who wears [a] kilt and if anybody don't listen to him, he beats them up.' Now, I was very worried – when I went to Stirling I report to Mr Duncan who was the Station Master and as I was learning the job I always kept looking back and Inspector … Joe Greesley says to me, 'I notice you keep looking round, what's the matter?' I say, 'I'm looking for the foreman who wears a kilt and is very hard.' He laughed. He said, 'There's nobody here bar two Tommies, because there's two foreman and they're both called Tommy.' And one was four foot six and the other one was six foot. So from there it set my mind at peace.

I was on the job for six weeks when the Station Master Mr Duncan come to me he says, 'I'm in trouble.' I said, 'Well I can't help you because I'm no passed out.' He said, 'Look, as you know, there's nobody for the Oban job because Guard Lyle has taken ill and nobody want to go to Oban.' I said, 'I'm quite willing to go but,' I says, 'I'm no passed out.' He says, 'Don't worry, come with me.' This was already arranged between him and Inspector Thornton who was the District Inspector, he was sitting waiting in his office for me. 'Now,' he says, 'I got you now. See how much you know.' So I went in his office, we were in there for two to three hour and he said to me, 'I've no doubt you're capable of doing the job. Would you do Mr Duncan a favour and go to Oban tomorrow?' I said, 'Yes, I will.' I was put on the job, I come out in the morning, it was a very very hard job because if you don't sort out the traffic parcel newspaper, because they were ... some ladies in the road, and if you don't deliver their paper you were in very serious trouble. I went on that job and I left Stirling 45 minutes late. Yet, I was at Oban ten minutes before my time. And everybody want to know how I did it. Well, the secret of that was, I used to come out half an hour before my time and set my van [where] the traffic properly should be and then as the London traffic arrived I used to put it aside, on the places, and all the important paper I used to put 'em aside and delivered them and ... these little small places that farmhouse and that I used to throw the paper off and kept the train moving, driver and I had a understanding, and I used to make up time. And everybody on that line was very happy, some of the station masters used to come out in their pyjamas and say, 'Oh, Mohammed, we were having a sleep, you're early.' 'Well,' I said, 'that's the way it goes.' And I stayed on the job for six months and I was very happy, and nobody liked Oban run but I did and the people in that area was very happy.

One day I was coming back from Oban and I stopped at Killin junction, and this gentleman came along and he says to me, 'You stop in Luib for three minutes. What was the reason for that?' I did not know who he was, I said, 'Sir, because from Taynuilt the driver came down fast and we had couple of minutes to wait in Luib, I could not leave before time because passengers will miss the train.' He never said anything, he went away. When

I went back the next day, the Station Master at Killin came to me and he said, 'What did you say to him yesterday?' I said, 'I just told him that we were running early so I could not leave before my time.' He said, 'Did you know who he was?' I said, 'No.' He said, 'He was the Director of LMS. If you had said the wrong thing you would have got sacked when you got to Stirling.' I said, 'Oh, thank you.' He said, 'He's very pleased with you and he hoped to meet you again.'

Well, I stayed [at] Stirling and while I was there I was booked to go to Edinburgh one day and as we passed Polmont, we stopped at Bo'ness junction and the signalman advised me that there's a lorry fell off the bridge at Linlithgow and we're gonna be some delay. I signed the book as per the rule, I came down to my passenger and I told them. Unknown to me that the gentleman, once again very tall gentleman, now I know he was Mr Carnegie of Transport Committee in Glasgow, he said to me that, 'I got to have a meeting in Edinburgh, very important meeting, can you pass a message that I'm on my way but will be delayed?' After standing at Bo'ness junction for ten to fifteen minutes, we moved off and the signalman told me that we would be going over the crossover onto the wrong line and past the obstruction at Linlithgow. But when we got there, the signal was clear and we would nae going to stop. So … I told the porter to phone Edinburgh and tell them that we're on our way and Mr Carnegie will be able to attend the meeting. We arrive in Edinburgh and Mr Carnegie thanked me and he went away. About a month later I was called into the Station Master's office and Mr Duncan says to me, 'Read this.' This was a letter from Mr Carnegie to Mr Killin, who was Superintendent [at] Perth, [about] how I performed my duty. That night, when I went to Edinburgh, every guard was looking at me, I was surprised – why? And one of the guards said, 'There come the pretty face, he gets a letter we don't.' I still do not understand what and one of the guard took me to that letter he says, 'That you?' I said, 'Yes.' He said, 'Well, we never had that kind of letter before.' I said, 'Well, I only did my job.' But few year later, when I got appointed Glasgow, every guard was looking at me again and they say, 'That's the same man who had the letter.' Apparently this letter was sent to all the guards' rooms and then the guards were told that if everyone done their job same as me, there'd be [a] different railway.

TWO PINTS
OF MILK

DAVID CREW + 1950s

A locomotive fireman in the Yorkshire area
remembers performing duties for the Royal Train

I WAS A FIREMAN ... and the foreman come and he said ... 'Oh tonight,' he says, 'you're not on your regular job,' he said, 'you've got the Royal Train.' Of course, you know your chest stood out, he said, 'You come in your clean overalls you know ... come clean and tidy like, your shoes shined and all that 'cos you're on the Royal Train.' So I says, 'Oh champion,' you know, fame at last...

I think we started about 10 o'clock at night and when we got there he, the foreman said, 'Now what you're doing, you're taking these two pint bottles of milk to Huddersfield and get the last train to Penistone, go passenger from Huddersfield to Penistone, but the train'll stop at Shepley and Shelley and you get off there and walk to Clayton West Junction and the Royal Train is in the sidings at Clayton West Junction. You relieve the fireman and driver on the Royal Train and stand there all night keeping the Royal Train warm and you haven't to make any noise and you're to pass these two bottles of milk to the detective on duty and in the morning … you've to just hook the Royal Train off when they get the other engine on the other end and that engine will take the Royal Train away and then you bring the engine back to the shed.' And when we got there, we did all this we got on the engine and the detective came up and he said, 'Now you haven't [to] make any noise when you're firing … you're to keep steam up but you haven't to make any noise shovelling coal and you haven't to rattle any fire irons,' and, 'All right then,' you know, and the Queen was in the train of course…

Yeah, she was the train when she was, well must have been when she was just the Queen actually, she's just new at it, you know and so we said, 'Oh okay like,' you know and of course you to get a shovel full of coal and carry it across the footplates and just put it in the fire box right gently so it didn't [make any noise], I mean when you was firing normally you used to bounce the shovel on the fire box door to make the coal go to the front you know but you'd to just lift it in and make no noise you see, so it didn't disturb the Queen and we did all this took the engine back and that was my Royal Train firing was that, just stood in sidings keeping the train warm, but we thought, you know, we were going to … be famous for driving the Royal Train, but we didn't actually move it at all.

Taking a Racehorse on the Train

Brian Connorton ✦ 1950s and 1960s

A jockey based at Newmarket, Suffolk,
remembers how he travelled to race meets

WE USED TO RACE AT — we used to get a horse box at
that time. We had ... it was a big outfit in Newmarket called
Hammonds, used to take your horses by ... [motorised] horse
box to the ... shorter meetings. And ... the first, the first ones of
these I think were the British Rail. They bought a fleet of six
horse boxes out, the big ones, six horses and we used to travel in
them quite a bit...

These six – they made the first big ones – the railway. They
were a maroon colour, and you would get six horses in any one
horse box. Which at that time was ... marvellous. Because it
used to be just two or three ... In the motorised boxes they were
just little, sort of dicky seat really ... as the horse was looking
over at you, you were sat in the dicky seat. And that was it. And
there'd be a bell for you to contact the driver in case there was
any problems with the horse. And you would ring [the] bell and
he'd pull up and say, 'What's the matter with you?'...

Nice big roomy boxes, much, much better than the motor
ones ... beautiful ... One of these railway boxes used to take two
horses, if needed. There would be one compartment behind
the horses. If you were travelling two they would be ... stood
together, alongside one another with their heads through the
top. At the back of these was a big area where they used to put
all your hay, straw, racing tack and all the gear there. That was
at the back of the horse. And ... the horses looked through this
gap in the carriage. And then there'd be a shelf underneath,
where everything you put there – you know like your sandwiches

and, you know, your vacuum flask. And there was a lovely big ...
settee arrangement for the lad to sit on. Through the little door
there at the top left hand side, and there was the loo next door.
All in the same ... box in the carriage ... marvellous it was...

Well a typical journey ... nowadays they go up the ramp into
a horse box, but you see with these horses and the ramps, they
were on the siding for the ... passenger like service – you know
– on a ... platform. So there wasn't a big ramp to climb up the
platform – the ramp laid down straight on the floor. And it was
inviting for a horse to go in ... sometimes you get horses that are
very difficult to put into these horse boxes – they don't want to go
up these big long ramps. But, the railway ... steam service didn't
have any problem like that; just inviting into the horse.
They was always well strawed up – plenty of straw on the floor
to make the horse, you know enjoy his travel and in he went.
The railway used to do this because they used to employ
two lads, to look after these horse boxes ... Or 'railway boxes'
we should call them I suppose. And, these two ex-racing lads
would make sure these ... boxes had everything, that was needed
for the horse. You know ... some water and all like that.
And ... they used to bring them in to the ... Newmarket horse
station at Warren Hill. There used to be an old heavyweight
Shire or two ... to pull these ... from the main line railway, down
this siding and into ... where the station is for the horses.
And this horse used to – the fella used to hook him onto this ...
this railway box ... Until they all got in. And then when they
used to come back they used to move them off and muck them
out and take them one at a time – these old horses used to pull
them away and two old racing lads with them, who used to tend
and care for these horses and do these things. Oh it was
marvellous. They used to go over the level crossing with the old
horses pulling it until they got to the siding ... and they used to
pull these in ... these horses one at a time ... And then that

would be the train like going for Doncaster or wherever the race meeting was … And then, as they all got loaded up – there used to be time of departure obviously, and you used to get there at least half an hour before departure. To make sure you were there and there was a crowd of people come … There'd be the head lad … and you know your mother and father, or … you know, girlfriend waving you off, 'Tata!' Off on the way to York and … there used to be just a train just for horses – horse box special, right … There'd be 10 or 12 horse boxes.

THE YOUNG ENTREPRENEURS OF POPPLETON

DICK SMITH ✦ 1960

Several young lads start their own business
at Poppleton Station in North Yorkshire

A GROUP OF US was very keen on buses and Barry Dane had an idea which combined this interest with a bit of money-raising. He started 'Poppleton General Transport' and built 'CML 1' (standing for 'Cartmaster Luggage'). Others of us joined in, with other carts built on old pram chassis; mine had the fleet number 'CBD 3' (Cartmaster, Type B, Drop-down door). The idea of the drop door was to make it easier to load heavy luggage. We used to meet trains at the station (sometimes buses too) and offer to carry luggage for travellers. In those days more people arrived at Poppleton with luggage, and fewer were met by friends with a car, so it was not such an unrewarding idea as it would be now. Barry pushed the bus idea further by fitting his cart with destination blinds. We were lucky that our then neighbour, Mr Kirk of 'The Kloof', had a spare garage opening directly onto Dikelands Lane which he allowed us to use.

We charged no fixed fee for the jobs, but invited contributions for a children's charity – I think the Children's Society, who gave us blue plastic imitation safes as collecting boxes.

Barry realised there were other possible sources of loads to carry, and built a 'low loader' which was really big; it had side members of 3" square timber, and steerable front wheels as it was so big. It needed a crew of three as one had to sit on to steer, and had no brakes so needed two people to slow it down when loaded. I can't remember what the wheels were, but they were probably not up to the job, as I remember we had problems with them. This 'CL 6' (Cartmaster Low-loader) was specially built for carrying peat from the Gardens' Guild store. A bale of peat fitted easily on the load platform, giving some idea of the size. The Gardens' Guild store at the time was in a garage just off the Green. Again, fewer people had access to a car, and as hatchbacks hadn't been invented, there was a niche for this kind of service.

I guess we kept it up for just a few months, probably from spring through to the Christmas holidays. At one stage I made a bracket for 'CBD 3' so I could put a bike light on the front, so we must have worked through some winter or autumn days. I don't know how much money we collected, but at one time we had a mention in the charity's magazine, complete with a photograph. I seem to remember we posed for photos on the station platform using empty suitcases, and at least one photo was a giveaway as it showed someone lifting a large case above his head.

We never had anything but kind support from people in the village, or indeed the train staff. Looking back, this is amazing but perhaps a tribute to the fact that as most people in the village would recognise most of us, they trusted us. I'm not sure youngsters today would be allowed to do this sort of thing without regulatory or insurance worries.

THE PASSWORD
IS COURAGE

CHARLES COOK ✦ 1962

*The former Public Affairs Manager for the Eastern Region of British
Railways describes how he aided the filming of a Dirk Bogarde feature*

AT ST PANCRAS ... that year [1962] when I came back
from doing a job ... the porter in the hall said to me, he said,
'There's a real beauty sitting waiting for you,' he said. 'Lovely
blond-haired woman in your office.' So I said, 'What?' He said,
'Yes,' he said, 'you go and see.' So I hared up the stairs at Pancras
– you know, this great winding staircase – and there was a lady
called Virginia Stone and she was the wife of Mr Stone, who was
a very eminent producer for MGM films. And she said, in a great
American voice, 'Oh hello, Mr Cook, I've been waiting for you.
We want to crash a train, set fire to a train, and we're making a
motion picture about a famous RSM in the British Army called
Charles Coward. And these are the things he did in Germany.'
So I said, 'Well, you know, well we can arrange all this.' And we
took – I took down all the notes and so on and what was required.
I said, 'Who's going to star?' So she said, 'Dirk Bogarde.' I went,
'Oh, lovely.' And this was the making of the film *The Password is
Courage* for MGM. And what we did, we organised the whole
thing at Scratchwood Sidings – which is now, of course,
Scratchwood service station at the beginning of the M1. And the
technicalities of setting trains on fire which you could put out
immediately afterwards without a scratch of damage to the train
was quite remarkable. Small charges were placed inside all these
trucks and things because Charles Coward had escaped from
German prison camps on no less than seventeen occasions.
And on every one he had organised – he was a real digger, he
was a sergeant major in the British Army – he organised these

lads in these prison camps to do all sorts of terrible things by expressing willingness to do work for the Germans – quite against the Geneva Convention and Lord knows what – and then turning it to advantage by setting fire to the place ... and so on. He set fire to the most major timber yard in Germany in this time, he exploded an ammunition train – and we had to concoct all this at Scratchwood Sidings. And a really exciting and marvellous time it was.

Well I took all this down and thank goodness by that time I was well-versed in the ramifications of railway departments and so I laid out all listing on great sheets of foolscap paper and said, 'Would the Divisional Engineer do this? And would the Chief Passenger Manager do this? And would you do that?' You know, and so on, right the way through, laying out this entire film. And I always remember ... Mr Cheetham at the Board ... was responsible for disposing of stock. So we sold MGM this locomotive which we then turned into a German locomotive of course with smoke-deflector plates on either side and iron crosses and other things stuck all over and what have you. And you couldn't have told that it was a British engine. And we did all sorts of things with this train. Anyway, the big thing was, I went to Cheetham and we charged, I figure – well I think it was £3,500 for this loco. And then I went to MGM and I said, 'Look, we've got this loco and – you know, we're going to transform it into a German loco but at the end sequence you want me to crash this down this 40-foot embankment at Scratchwood?' So they said, 'Yes, that's right.' So I said, 'Well, you do realise that we can never recover it because it's an embankment and we can't have cranes with outriggers on because they haven't got anywhere to hold the weight.' I said, 'You realise, there's a hundred tons of loco there?' 'Oh, well, once we've got it we don't want it any more. You can sell it for scrap.' So I went back to Cheetham and I said, 'Look, we can sell this for scrap.' So, we got the price of £3,500 pounds for the locomotive and after the film was completed we sold the loco for £5,000 for scrap, to be cut up on site.

Anyway, this film was jolly good and I always remember, during the filming Dirk Bogarde was a gem, he really was. And he had his fortieth birthday during this – the filming on this location. And he sported everybody a champagne meal – a superb waitress-served champagne meal on the site – it was really wonderful … I was just liaising with him, of course, and that – but he was no problem at all.

And then we had this train to set on fire … we had to simulate this. And these great funnels of steel were put in these wagons, with small charges and balsa wood and stuff like that and propane gas. And then, on the blind side, away from the cameras, great hoses and electric cables were festooned all the way down this 40-wagon train so that, as it came along, it would blow up. And this was done and they put jelly all over the sides of the trains and it really makes a most impressive blaze and all this was going on – we had the fire engine and tenders, we'd arranged this with the fire brigade and what have you and of course, when we said, 'Right, all done, you can put the fire out now,' the fire brigade they said, 'Oh, we haven't got any water.' And so, they rushed a tender up there and managed to get the fire put out. But the incredible thing, there wasn't a scar on the train, no. Well then the next thing was to … simulate Charles Coward tearing up the floorboards in one of the prisoners' vans, now he was going to escape through the floor when the train slowed down. And the – apparently he was clapped into jail for this in Germany because the guard of the train suddenly saw floorboards dropping in the track and so he leant out, you see, and blew this hooter they have in Germany, and waved his arms about and the train came to a stand and the guard of the train came along and saw these holes in the floor and said, 'What made that hole?' And at which the answer apparently from Charles Coward, which was a genuine answer, he said, 'Mice.' The Germans didn't think it was funny at all. Anyway, they clapped him in irons.

We had to finally crash this train down the embankment – with all these wagons on the back of it and so on. And Dirk Bogarde rushes down, dressed as a German in a German officer's uniform, you see, and waving his arms about and saying, 'Schnell, schnell,' you know, and all this sort of thing to the guards … Well we staged this by putting a – got the civil engineer to put in a disguised switch right at the end of this embankment and it was – we measured it was 44 feet down. And the camera people came along and they said, 'We got one chance on this. So, come on Mr Cook!' And they got me out here, he said, 'Where do you think that loco's gonna land?' So I said, 'Well, I don't know, I suppose it'll be about there,' I said. 'Right,' they said, 'Dig in the camera there.' He put this camera worth about five thousand quid or something … about ten feet from where the locomotive landed. And he had five cameras on this to capture the moment. And we brought in a 0-6-0 – one of the old … steam engines. Anyway, that was to get it a good push and we got it up to about, oh, 40-odd miles an hour and then the crew jumped off and along it came under its own power, going like mad – I got some film of this I took on an eight millimetre camera because I wasn't gonna miss that. And then suddenly it hit this switch and toppled over, rolled over three times and then came up on its wheels. And all these trucks with the kinetic energy of having been shot along at 40 miles an hour all came tumbling down as being smashed to pieces. And it really was a terrible looking railway accident.

PREPARING FOR ROYAL VISITORS

STEWART CURRIE ✦ 1960s

A British Railways civil engineer
describes a mishap before a royal visit

WE HAD AN ARRIVAL in [Glasgow] Central Station, where the carpet was set up and everything and we had two arrivals – it was on a Friday. And the train came in about eleven in the morning and the Queen and Duke of Edinburgh and everybody got off and everybody was quite happy and it all worked out all right. Then they came back onto the train to change for an evening engagement – they'd towed it out to some siding on the south side and then they brought the train back and I made the fatal mistake of saying, 'Well, it's the same train, we can't go wrong this time – same red carpet, same place, no problems.' And the train came in and missed the red carpet by – it stopped short of the red carpet by about 50 feet. And the reason for that was that the lookout man, who stood with a flag down where the locomotives should stop to indicate this had been paid between the first and the second arrival and had retired to a local hostelry, and came back, clutching a red flag saying, 'I've got to stop the Royal Train,' and was promptly arrested – taken off by the British Transport police. So there was nobody there when the train came in and the driver very wisely stopped short rather than too far. Fortunately Smith was the Station master in Central at the time and an old, very old hand, he just stepped forward very quickly when he saw what had happened and just shouted, 'Keep all the doors shut.' And we just moved the train up. And I was dragged before [the General Manager] after the event, 'If you continue to make blunders of this magnitude, Currie, you won't be a District Engineer much longer.'

There was another one where we had about three or three or four visits – this was in Scotland. We started off at Dumfries I think it was and then they motored all round the south west and rejoined the train at Motherwell. So, when they had finished arriving at Dumfries, I had two lorries to pick up all the flowers and took them up and we put them out in Motherwell … When they got on … we took them again and put them in a van and stuck them on the back of the Royal Train to go to Inverness. And they got in very early in the morning so they were able to unload them again and put them up again. Somebody tipped off the Duke of Edinburgh what we were doing. He thought this was a great joke 'cos there was potted palms in this lot and he came out and [the General Manager] was meeting him again at Inverness and he … took one look and he'd been primed, I reckon, and he said, 'Good God, not these damn palms again!'

MEMORIES OF
DR BEECHING

ANDREW ELLIOTT ✦ 1963–1964

A rail enthusiast remembers the effect
of the Beeching Axe on his childhood

WHAT DID DOCTOR BEECHING ever do for us? Well, what he did for me personally was this: he imbued me with a sense of loss for the familiar world of my childhood; he taught me to distrust authority; and, by default, he gave me a lifelong interest in the geography and economy of the British Isles.

As a six year old I had witnessed the closure of the Yorkshire coastal railway, which had once run along the cliff tops from Staithes to Whitby. I can remember family days at the seaside: looking out from the carriage windows – the maroon, suburban, slam door, non-corridor carriages – as the train crossed the viaducts at Sandsend; the grey North Sea waves rolling in beneath the drumming train wheels. I remember the nights, when the lights of inshore fishing boats were strung out over Runswick Bay as we made our way home. And I can still vividly remember the long uphill walks to West Cliff Station with weary legs, and with sandals filled with sand.

In 1963, when the Beeching Report was made public, I was an eleven year old. I had seen the local engine sheds at Stockton being closed, and the engines moved away. I was aware of the then recent closure of the old South Durham and Lancashire Union Railway – the line which had linked the industries of Teesside with the shipyards of Barrow in Furness, Birkenhead and Belfast; and which crossed the Lake District, linking the Steelworks of Teesside with those of Workington.

I was aware that new diesel engines had been appearing, sometimes replacing the North Eastern Pacifics on the Newcastle to London services – I had often heard the steam engine on the 23.49 sleeper train, whistling as it passed Stockton Bank signal box and rattling beneath the big gantry at the north end of Stockton marshalling yards. On clear nights, it was possible to look out across the nearby fields and to see the heated dot of the engine's fire box, drawing a bead of red light along the horizon in the dark.

I was very aware that things were changing, but the Beeching Report came as a shock to us all: it was difficult to believe that the intended closures could possibly be so draconian. On television there were studio discussions about 'pruning dead wood' and 'economic necessity' – but the bottom line was that many much-loved railways would be closed, and that the closures would begin very soon; and that there was nothing that any of us could do to stop these things happening: it seemed to us that the intended closures were inevitable, *a fait accompli.*

Fifty years later, I can see that, as a nationalised industry, British Railways – as they were then called – had no pressure group to stand up for them, and that there was a desire, on behalf of the then government, to build new roads – which would both aid the building industry and generate income from taxes on fuel and on vehicle licences. It is possibly extremely significant that the then Minister of Transport was the part-owner of a road building company: something which a casual glance might perceive as having been an obvious conflict of interests. ...

It's interesting now to view the implications of the Beeching Closures from a wider perspective, and to speculate on the immediate and the long term consequences which they eventually and inevitably brought about. ...

Towards the end of August 1964, I sat on the stone parapet of the roadbridge over the Stockton to Newcastle line, watching the last steam-hauled special trains returning from York Races. Two V2s and an A3, 'St. Simon', came up Stockton Bank, glistening bright green in the evening sunlight, with the red paint and the window glasses flashing bright along the sides of the carriages, where the orange sun glittered and sparkled. It struck me then that I might be seeing these things for the very last time: I decided that I would take my savings – of almost one pound – and use the money to buy a one week Rover ticket, with which I would visit the local railways that were due for imminent closure.

During that one week I crammed in as much travel as I could manage. Most mornings saw me taking the early Darlington train from Thornaby station, the 08.15, from memory – because this was a return working of the 'very early' Saltburn newspaper/parcels train, and it always produced a steam engine, one of Darlington's tank engines – often 42085, which is now preserved on the Lakeside and Haverthwaite Railway. Very occasionally the train would produce one of the very last V3s, and I saw 67690 on it in the December of 1964 – very late in the day for such an engine.

From Darlington, I travelled along the western branch lines which Doctor Beeching had selected for closure: the lines to Richmond, to Barnard Castle, to Middleton in Teesdale, and to Crook – behind Fowler tank 42405. On the remaining two days, I travelled to Whitby – along the Esk Valley Line, where a B1 was waiting in the bay, ready to go back to Malton, along what is now the North Yorkshire Moors Railway: and to Hartlepool, where the shed still owned a J72 shunting engine and the yard was crammed with well-used freight engines: Q6s, K1s, 'Austerities' – and a single, grubby and 'run-down' looking V2. ...

In my own small way I celebrate 'what once was' by walking along the old railway lines and remembering how things used to be. And along the way I pass cyclists and joggers and dog walkers, and often stop to exchange a word about how civilised the world was fifty years ago – when it was possible to travel comfortably to most corners of the United Kingdom, both in reasonable comfort and at an affordable price.

The Isle of Wight and the Beeching Axe

Jack Richards ✦ 1963

A petitioner against Dr Beeching's Axe on the Isle of Wight describes the efforts of the island's Railway Retention Society

THE BEECHING PLAN envisaged closing down the entire network with the exception of a shuttle down the pier from the ferry to the Esplanade Station to connect with buses.

The bus company gave notice to BR that it could not manage the huge numbers of Saturday visitors at the cramped location. Alternative plans to extend to a new bus station at St John's Road station were put forward, but the bus company was luke warm. This placed BR in a dilemma as it had to be able to convince the TUCC that alternatives were available.

Despite this BR ploughed on insisting that the buses could manage – convincing no one, bus company included.

I was involved in the Railway Retention Society which was formed on the Isle of Wight. I was only sixteen at the time, but I helped with petitions.

The Society and the County Council together demolished the financial case for the closure of the Ryde to Ventnor line. It transpired that BR had only counted revenue from the local stations and had ignored the bulk of the income from the vast numbers of incoming passengers. It was pointed out that a closure case could be made for Waterloo if only outgoing revenue was counted.

There were huge public meetings and massive protests. It emerged that it was overall policy under the plan to close seaside branches regardless of viability. The Ventnor route was in profit, but that didn't matter.

In the end, the TUCC recommended that the Ryde–Ventnor route should be spared as it would cause exceptional hardship. The report landed on Labour's Minister of Transport Tom Fraser's desk with two civil servants' views. One wanted to close the lot and the other wanted to retain Ryde–Ventnor. He struck a deal. Keep Ryde–Shanklin open and close to Ventnor – which ruined the town's economy overnight and it has never recovered.

Much of this information was obtained when I worked on the campaign to re-open the Ventnor section in the 1990s. BR was dismayed by the decision – they either wanted complete closure or to retain the whole line. It would only be viable as a complete route.

THE END OF
A GOLDEN AGE

RICHARD SPENDLOVE MBE ◆ 1960s

The regional and local radio presenter and producer created and co-wrote (with David Croft) the BBC comedy series Oh Doctor Beeching!

I STARTED ON the railways in 1954, as a box boy in a signal box near Nottingham. I worked in there until I was called up to do National Service in the middle of 1959. When I came out about two years later, I went back straight on to the railway, began as a trainee signalman and then forged my way through the various signalling grades, from the lower grades to the senior grade in 17 months … I applied for a job as a Station Master and I was appointed a Relief Station Master at Cambridge … there was a higher grade Relief Station Master at Ely, which I took and then … I spent a little bit of time then as the Assistant Area Manager at Ely…

I think that it's fair to say that the work that [Beeching] did, while it effectively decimated the system, also decimated the morale of the people who worked on it because there were so many stations and signal boxes and places closed and so many jobs went.

I mean, for instance, when they made the station masters redundant. I was one of 26 Relief Station Masters at Cambridge and 26 of us were made redundant in one afternoon. So on the basis of that, the morale went completely down the chute – there is no question about that at all. It was inevitable that it would because so many of these people had been on the railways so long that they had been convinced – and indeed told – that provided they behaved themselves, they had jobs for life and then all of a sudden, they sent this chairman of ICI in who chopped the thing to pieces. ...

Certainly there were stations that were closed which should never ever, under any circumstances on God's earth have been closed. If we just take this area in particular, if you take Wisbech. Wisbech is a relatively large town and needed a railway station – that was closed. If you take Haverhill, that was at that time a relatively quiet station and was not doing massive business. It was keeping itself going, but at the time that it was closed, it was weeks away from becoming a London overspill town and before you knew where you were, you couldn't move in the town for people. The population grew by thousands in weeks and they'd taken the station away! Saffron Walden was another case in point. Now I happened to be at Saffron Walden the week that it closed and the week that it closed – this was a station that had two signalmen, a couple of porters and a Station Master – it took 5,000 pounds worth of parcel traffic, let alone anything else and it was a feeding branch line to Audley End station, which was the main line to Liverpool St.

One of the most alarming aspects of the whole affair was the speed at which the stations were closed and the shocking lack of respect shown for railway installations that had stood for over a hundred years as a shining example of British ingenuity and enterprise. To give you some idea of the way these people worked ... The night they had closed Saffron Walden, they ripped the lines up with such indecent haste ... that in actual fact, they left a carriage in the Saffron Walden siding platform at Audley End with no railway lines to get it out from!

THE TRAVELLING
POST OFFICE

COLIN MELLISH ✦ 1965 ONWARDS

*A worker on the Travelling Post Office (TPO) trains recalls
the experience of sorting the post from Euston to Carlisle*

MY FIRST TRIP on the train was actually in November and
I'll never forget, it was on the late train which was the north-west
train ... mainly run from Euston to Carlisle. It terminated in
Carlisle, it never used to go through to Scotland and ... was
mainly an English train, it sorted out the English counties of the
north-west ... and maybe Southern Scotland but never used to
go any further ... it was cold, it was freezing and we got stuck
half way up Shap [incline] and in a snow and I've never seen, I'd
never seen snow like it before ... we looked out the door and
there was twelve-foot drifts either side of us and it was absolutely
atrocious and we had, at the time, we had the ... steam pipes
going across the top and no electric heating and of course it was
absolutely freezing 'cos the steam pipes had actually frozen up as
well ... that first, very first trip, I believe we got into Carlisle
about four or five hours late and it was ... we was all falling
about in Carlisle, the streets were full of ice, it hardly ever snows
in Carlisle, but it does get very icy and the pavements are like a
skating rink and ... we'd never seen anything like it ... it was [an]
unbelievable trip.

If we was on the early train which was the down special
Travelling Post Office – we'd start work at around about 7.15
and then we'd work in the station till 8.25, till the train pulled out
and then we'd be off on our way to Carlisle, we'd be sorting
letters all the way. There were twelve sorting coaches and the
work was more than we could handle in those days. We were
working from the time we got on the train really to the time we

got off in Carlisle and sometimes we never used to quite finish it because there was so much of it.

We used to pick up letters on the way … at Hemel Hempstead … and Leighton Buzzard and places like that and then we'd drop them off further down the line. The postman who was at the back of the train used to look out of the train and he'd know every sort of mark and house and tree and whatever little mark they might have for the apparatus – it's called the apparatus – and they used to look out of the train and they'd see a certain point, they count the number of bridges and beats on the wheels … before the track was welded they used to count the beats of the wheels and then they'd look out for the mark on the way … the mark might be for that particular pickup, he'd look out of the window and … he'd count these bits and pieces and then, where the pickup point was there was a white board on the side of the track, soon as he saw the white board … he used to … push the lever down on the side of the train, and this net used to come out and it'd take … maybe 30 seconds to a minute after that before it picked up the actual mail bags and they, the mail bags, were actually wrapped in very thick leather casings – they were a quarter of an inch thick … weighed 60 pound on their own, these … pouches … you used to wrap about three or four mail bags in 'em but there was nothing allowed in them that was fragile, the fragile used to have go a different route.

When the pouches came in, the postman used to open them up, there were fixed straps on 'em and they used to have to undo the straps. It was quite a business undoing the straps and they used to pick out the four mail bags, the postman did, what was in each pouch and then maybe there might be something like six pouches coming in … They'd sort the bags into which coach they had go into and they'd bring the bags through the whole train while it was going along at about 90 miles hour … they'd walk through the train with these bags on their backs. They was quite weighty bags of course and they'd drop off the bags in whichever coach they needed to be sorted in, as on the down special travelling post office there was eight divisions of … Scotch mail only and they used to have to drop off the bags on to the eight divisions – all different Scottish counties and areas … they had to be sorted first.

It was really by memory … it was really experience that counted on sorting those days, it was sorting into counties not numbers like they do these [days] … you had to memorise, say a place called Kilbarchan, which was in Renfrewshire. If it never had the county town on it you had to know where Kilbarchan actually went to … which sorting office sorted it. If we got the odd letter you didn't know, you put it to one side and someone with more experience would come through and say, 'What you got there … mate?' … he'd look through and say, 'That goes to so-and-so, this one goes over there and that one goes to St Johnston, this one goes to Perth and that one goes to Stirling and this one goes to Thurso,' and so on.

Refreshments well … even on the old coaches there was a water boiler and an oven. You could put your pies in the oven, you could warm things up, but it never actually used to cook 'em, it used to sort of just warm them up for you and the urn used to fill up … with water from the tank … which was above on the roof of the … sorting coach just above where the toilet was … and it used to draw water from the tank above and in those days they never had a filter on 'em – they only put the filters on at a later date so you used to get the water from the tank which was full of whatever might have been in it after they'd … they'd obviously never used to disinfect it every night I wouldn't imagine or clean it out … they used to just fill it up with water. And of course you never knew what you was getting in this water, sometimes the tea you made with it tasted really awful. Sometimes there was diesel fumes in the stuff and it was horrible … But this urn that used to boil up the water as it was going along ... the wheels used to turn a dynamo I suppose ... used to heat up an element in the ... urn itself ... it used to take quite a time, about an hour before you could even get any hot water out of it ... you start making the tea and you're doing about 90 miles an hour and you go across a set of points and the train starts to rock ... and of course you can quite easily ... scald yourself with it ... It was quite a dangerous process actually making tea on a train.

Sometimes some people used to bring kippers on and lay them on the steam pipe above, as the ovens weren't very efficient and you used to get the smell of kippers ... wafting all through the train all night long and it was horrible smell ... it used to stink on there like a fish train ... and in the summer on the down special TPO there was about three or four nets [to] collect the pouches in ... but you only need to use one of them so the others we used as a fridge, they used to put their ... milk in it, and their kippers in it and their fish they'd bought up north in it, they used to open up the door and put it in the net, then of course this train'd be going along with a load of fish in the net and maybe some milk and ... what was in these nets certainly wasn't mail.

NEW BEGINNINGS

1968–1990s

The slimmed-down and 'modernised' British Rail set about improving its public image. The 'Inter-City' brand with its highly successful advertising campaign halted the public's steady drift away from rail travel, and the introduction of new liner trains using centralised container distribution depots began to reverse the lacklustre rail-freight industry.

Rural railways that survived the 1960s cull soon found themselves reduced to operating a 'bus' service with onboard conductor/guards and unstaffed stations, and many survived with only Government subsidies, their social need outweighing their profitability.

The 1970s saw the completion of many electrification schemes and the introduction of the highly successful and long-lived HST 125s, which are still in service today.

One dream of the Victorian railway builders eventually saw the light of day when construction of the Channel Tunnel started in 1988. It took six years to build, with a cost overrun of 80 per cent, but today it provides a much-needed high-speed link with the Continent. William Barlow's magnificent St Pancras station, once threatened with demolition in the 'enlightened' 1960s, has since been reborn as the gateway to Europe.

By 1990, the Government had sold off nearly all of Britain's state-owned industries except the railways. The countdown to privatisation had begun and the Railways Act of 1993 sealed the fate of the railways as they were broken up piecemeal. Despite fragmenting and ridding themselves of the national rail network, successive governments still have to dig deep to keep them running.

ILKLEY MOOR
BAHT'AT

BILL ADDY ✦ 1970s

*Speaking in the 2000s, a driver remembers the
unintended effect of his engine's whistle*

I READ IN the *Yorkshire Evening Post*, not a long time ago, this
person ... remembers there must have been one particular
engine driver who was always when ... using his whistle ... was
playing 'Ilkley Moor Baht'at,' and I realised what he was talking
about was me. There is a code of whistles and every driver in
those days, when you come to stand at a signal, you have to
whistle [to] say where you want to go at the next junction.
There's a different whistle for if you're on the main line, it's one
long one [and] if you want to go to the right at the next junction
it's a long and a short and so on ... If you want to attract the
signalman's attention for line-side fires, there's a code [for] that,
and if you want to attract attention I used to whistle 'Ilkley Moor
Baht'at' and with an old steam engine that was quite easy –
eventually we got reported for being noisy...

Now this was while I was at Farnley and even with a horn it
isn't easy, but with a bit of skill and at the same time as I whistled
there's a row of houses and [at] the first house the lady used to
come out every time and stand at the bottom of the garden and
wave to me like mad from quite a distance away ... every day,
every time I passed, I never used to hesitate, I used to whistle
'Ilkley Moor Baht'at' and out she would come without fail and
quite often at weekends, there'd be her husband with her...

There's times when I used to work the Deltics instead of a
high speed, you can't do anything on the high speed train but
with the Deltics at this junction, just as you come out of
Doncaster, I forget the name, I used to whistle again for this

crossing … right up to leaving work, to retiring, I used to whistle and this lady used to always fetch her family out, there was quite a gang of them and they used to wave like mad, and I thought, 'Well blimey.' … the only thing I can think is that that lady in each case she must have had some Yorkshire connections … it's one of the nice parts about my life on the railway.

High Speed Trains: Testing for Noise

Geoff Page + 1970s

A former passenger guard at Hatfield and King's Cross remembers the introduction of the High Speed Trains (HSTs)

WHEN THE HSTs came in that was a very good line to work on because they were very speedy and also fairly punctual. The only thing wrong, they were very noisy, the HSTs, the diesel engine, and the diesel, the driver could get through from the cab, right through into the train, same as they did in the 'Flying Scotsman' or something like that I think it was, anyway, so there was a passage way. I went through once into there and once you get, open the door to go through there is a heck of a roar and it's very narrow, it's like getting down in a submarine I should imagine, there's about as much room to, a little narrow passage and then eventually go through another door into the driver's cab. Well, one day I had somebody on the train that said he was a representative, he was testing for noise or something on the diesels, so I said, 'Okay.' But he said, 'I'd like to go through to the driver.' So on them days I think I could get through to the driver on the phone if I remember right, so I rung him up and I told him who was on the train and he wanted to come through to test … how many decibels or something of the engine compartment

... I said, 'Now before we go through, there's going to be a heck of a noise so be prepared.' So ... we opened the door, he got into there and the first thing that flew up straight was his tie! ... he obviously didn't realise there was so much noise, but he eventually went through and had a chat to the driver, so those HSTs were very noisy but they were very powerful.

ADVENTURES IN THE TYPING POOL

CHRISTINE MCMILLAN ✦ 1970s

A partially sighted typist working for
British Railways remembers her first years at work

I NEVER ACTUALLY CONSIDERED working for the railway. When I came to leave school, the choices weren't terribly great. For one thing I don't think that they expected girls to have a career and for another thing people with a visual impairment, at least partially sighted people, weren't given the same opportunities as the blind, because the blind, particularly the boys, could go into clergy, they could go into teaching, they could do physiotherapy, but you needed a lot more qualifications than I had got. If you weren't terribly bright you went and worked in a factory. But I was in the grammar stream and if you got O levels then they thought you'd stay on and do A levels, well I didn't get high enough grades and the options were working in the Civil Service. And so they decided that I would go to the ordinary tech college here in Reading and I would do a secretarial course. Anyway, I did that and when it came to leaving college I still didn't know what I wanted to do. So eventually I'd applied for all sorts of jobs, I did a bit of temping, which was equally useless because I didn't have the skills, I didn't have the maturity.

The disablement assessment officer didn't really know what to do with me. And eventually Dad said, 'Well shall I ask if there's a job for you on the railways?' I must have said, 'Yes, all right,' or he did it without telling me. I was told to go up to Paddington for an interview as an audio typist. So I got on the train and I went up to Paddington. Whether I was the first visually impaired person they had come across, I don't know, nobody's ever told me, but I was placed in the typing pool in the General Manager's office and off we went.

The years I was actually there were from 1970–1979, and things changed a great deal over that time. When I first arrived, we were treated as little girls and we were not allowed to talk to the people we worked for. They certainly weren't allowed to come up to our desks and talk to us ... all our communication was via the telephone and we had to ask to use the telephone. But that was only after the supervisor had said that we could do. We weren't allowed to have any initiative of ourselves. It was she or the deputy that had to listen to any queries we had and if they couldn't get them then we were allowed to use the telephone. I can only even remember talking to two women in all that time, but slowly over that time things changed. Now I don't know why, or whether it was just that we were all teenagers of the sixties and we were not going to be dictated to, but as more younger men arrived so the older ones had to give way...

I think that they could obviously see something was different and word must have gone around the GMO's office that there was something wrong with this person. Although I knew that I didn't look any different and apart from a short time of using a white stick, nobody could tell by looking at me. But men used to talk to me and ask me questions and eventually I committed the heinous crime [of] having a boyfriend on the railway.

When I first went there, everybody wore suits, dresses, we didn't wear trousers ... but eventually there were one or two other people from railway families whose fathers were guards, drivers, and the like … and obviously they'd grown up in the sixties fashions and they wanted to wear them to work. So mini skirts started to appear, jeans started to appear. The supervisor, I seem to remember, wore trousers so I tried doing it, my father wouldn't let me, wasn't done at Reading, and I wasn't going to do it and he didn't care if I got cold on the train I was not going out of the door with trousers on. Few rebellions in our household, but I wasn't allowed to and I didn't. It was a long time before I wore trousers.

ST PANCRAS: COME FRIENDLY BOMBS

IAN KRAUSE ✦ 1971–1972

*Now a TV Producer, Ian Krause remembers his
time as a booking clerk at St Pancras Station*

AS I SUP A PINT of Betjeman Bitter in the luxurious surroundings of the 'new' St Pancras, I do wonder what John Betjeman would have made of the place if he'd actually had to work there, rather than merely extolling its architectural worth. Work there I did … and, even now, it seems like a lifetime sentence. I was … a booking clerk. I didn't want to be a booking clerk, I wanted to be a TV director. But the BBC had other ideas, so I figured that the travel perks of working for BR outweighed the negatives. Thus, along with a motley collection of Irishmen (split evenly between south and north), I checked into the wonderfully ornate, George Gilbert Scott-designed booking office. Wonderfully ornate from the outside, but an accident waiting to happen inside, with a naked gas jet permanently breathing fire from the wall of the season-ticket office.

There were three shifts – 06.00 to 14.00, 14.00 to 22.00, and the graveyard night shift from 22.00 to 06.00. If somebody failed to turn in for their shift, you just carried on working. And that happened regularly, particularly on St Patrick's Day or other vital dates (of which there seemed to be many) in the Irish calendar. My first turn was the 06.00 one, and, as the new boy, it fell to me to shut down the ladies' loos at 12.00 in order to empty the pre-decimal sixpences from the slot machines on the toilet doors. Twenty minutes later, I would climb the steps to be greeted by stares of universal hatred from the waiting mob. It was then that I realised just how far down the pecking order I was destined to be.

The St Pancras hierarchy was quite rigid. Top of the pile was the station master — bowler hat, clipped white hair, military bearing. In charge of the ticket office was — a taciturn Irishman who I never saw smile in my entire sojourn there. Mind you, given the competence of some of his workforce, I'm not surprised. And then there were the rest of us. We were still selling the old Edmondson card tickets when I started. At the end of each shift, you had to balance your own books (huge ledgers), and if you were more than £5 out, then it was an official reprimand, and a deduction from your wages. Friday afternoons would be pandemonium, with takings of thousands of pounds at each window, but they paled into insignificance beside the dreaded Saturday football excursions. The nightmare game was Millwall/Luton, when gangs of supporters would try and nick their money back from the counter as you turned to get the tickets, with the railway police gazing benignly on.

The night shift was, in theory, a doddle. The last train left at 23.55, you shut the window, balanced all the day's takings, and curled up on the counter until 05.30 when the office re-opened. Unfortunately, the IRA had other ideas, and most nights were spent shivering on Euston Road, while the police ransacked the left-luggage lockers for explosives. But the job had its perks, not least the use of Chiltern Green station house, together with a motley collection of rats and spiders, for £3.27 a week. And there were moments to savour, such as the day when a well-known sports journalist arrived with a first-class travel warrant to Nottingham and demanded that his blonde assistant be added to it. After threatening to get me sacked when I declined, he beat a hasty retreat in the face of Her Majesty's Constabulary's offer to feel his collar. And there was the Sunday morning when an Indian gentleman arrived at 07.00 wanting a ticket to 'Beddeford'. Bedford or Bradford? He spoke no English and me no Urdu, but we eventually decided on Bradford. At 20.00 that evening (my replacement had failed to show), he returned with a scrap of paper. Bideford. In Devon. No train from Waterloo until tomorrow. But at least the Travelling Ticket Collector (also an Indian, who was writing a book on Moral Philosophy in his spare time) had taken pity, and we refunded the ticket money.

A VERY
ROYAL OCCASION

TREVOR ADAMS + 1981

*A British Railways manager at Waterloo
recalls the day he met royalty*

ONE OF THE BIG things that I was involved in there was the wedding of Princess Diana and Prince Charles. This was in 1981, and the plan was that Diana and Charles would travel by train from Waterloo to Romsey where they were going to spend the first part of their honeymoon at the home of the Mountbattens at Romsey. There was a lot of pre-planning obviously, I was well involved with the Palace ... we had a rehearsal on the Sunday morning. The wedding was the 29th of July, the Wednesday, and the rehearsal took place on Sunday the 26th of July and we were there fairly early in the morning – an early start – and again we had a closed carriage instead of the open landau that would be used on the Wednesday, we had troops all over the place, we had television cameras who were getting their sight lines ready – it was a good job we did have the rehearsal because the cameras were set up in one place for the world to see Diana getting out of her carriage – or Diana and Charles getting out of the carriage – and at the rehearsal it transpired that there would be eight horses right in front of the television cameras and the world's view would have been the rear end of eight horses. But that's what rehearsals are for.

Rehearsal I think would start at six o'clock on the Sunday morning and it included the procession from Buckingham Palace and so on, so we had that run through. I remember we had the Lord Chamberlain in attendance, and the Controller of the Household and equerries and the Master of the Horse and they were all there with tape measures and stopwatches and running through the arrangements. So that was the Sunday morning. On the Wednesday, the day of the wedding itself, the wedding as people remember was in St Paul's Cathedral, and I went with a small railway party over to the Charing Cross Hotel, and we watched the procession go by along the Strand, both to St Paul's and back from St Paul's to Buckingham Palace and then everybody else went home of the small railway group that we had there … except me and I started work. And I went to Waterloo to make sure that things were right. We'd unrolled a huge red carpet – the trouble was that as people walked on it, it left heavy footprints and we had people there with – we didn't have a vacuum cleaner – we had people with a stiff broom who were there to lift up the pile of the carpet because the problem was that with the television cameras it showed the footprints in the pile of the carpet, I remember that. But anyway, we got to the stage where we had the message from the police that the … procession had left Buckingham Palace, the royal couple had waved farewell to the Queen and the rest of the guests after the wedding breakfast, it was a bit hair raising because – I think it was at 3.30 the train and at 3.30 they were just about leaving Buckingham Palace and it wasn't good to have a late start on a train but – never mind, we held the train, obviously, waiting passengers, and I stood at the end of the red carpet and through the main arch of Waterloo station came the sound of people cheering and then turning the corner I could see the open landau being drawn by the horses. They got near, stopped right at the end of the carpet and Diana came out of the carriage, Princess Diana, and – followed by Prince Charles – and … we spoke, I welcomed her to Waterloo and a few other words. Charles said farewell to his – and I presume a thank you to his staff – and left me chatting to Diana for a couple of minutes, and then Prince Charles rejoined us and I introduced both of them to the General Manager and walked them the very short distance across the platform in to the Royal Train … the train drew out on its way to Romsey. I'm told it arrived at Romsey exactly on time, but there was a good excuse for the late start that day. But again, a tremendous day because the day didn't end there for the station staff in particular, the station staff at Waterloo were marvellous, we had the station absolutely full but the mess that was left behind to be cleared up afterwards only you can – I'm sure you can appreciate. But there were, you know, there were interesting things happening behind the scenes. The security side of course was extremely important, and the liaison with the security services – the police in particular – because there were threats or the possibility of threats from the IRA and so that was a worry but the police dealt with it absolutely magnificently, and the other thing of course is that passengers – people were trying to see the Royal Train … we had to keep people away and we even had people jumping on trains to travel out, hoping that they would parallel with the Royal Train on the way out of Waterloo and they kept jumping on and off because … their plans went wrong when the royal procession arrived late … it was quite an interesting time. But all was successful and away the Train went and a wonderful day and I had a wonderful message back from the Royal Household to say how pleased they were that things had gone so well.

Train Driving: Women's Work

Ann Henderson ✦ 1980s

*An engine driver in Scotland recalls her
experiences on the railway*

THERE DEFINITELY WAS a view amongst some of the drivers – not, not all of the drivers, some of the drivers and some of the inspectors – that it wasn't a job for a woman. But, again, some of the things that were problems, like perhaps the toilet facilities – I used to always get agitated about this earlier on in my railway career when I thought some of the women just talked about toilets all the time and I didn't want to be one of those women so I didn't but, I've got to say, when I became a freight guard it did become a bit of an issue because at most of the yards there were no toilet facilities and if there were there was only one and you had to get someone to hold the door, watch the door, and, you know, there were a whole lot of issues. It did become … something that we had to speak about sometimes.

Anyway, so there were all these kind of issues to deal with, and it was a heavier job, definitely a heavier job and you much

– you had to have a far greater understanding of railway workings and obviously freight traffic was more frequently shunted from place to place or ... run off the main line to ... allow the passenger trains priority and things like that so I've got a much better grasp of the way the railway worked and there were a lot of things I really liked about it and I know some of the freight guards. The way it worked in Queen Street [Glasgow] was promotion to the passenger link was automatic ... it was done through seniority at that time, it isn't any more because of the break-up of the industry and changes in what the unions have negotiated but it was at that time, and ... I knew some of the older freight guards who just like loved being freight guards and ... you know, opted not to go into the passenger link when their turn came up and they stayed on the freight. That changed, one of the knock-on effects of the train crew agreement was to shake all that up and I know that a number of the men felt, you know, [they] had no choice but to go into passenger jobs and they really were miserable doing them, didn't like them, weren't – not to say they weren't good with the public but they didn't want to work with the public, they wanted to work with freight wagons, you know, and I always thought it was kind of a shame because it changed, it didn't make the best of everybody's kind of skills and expertise ... and again in the moving, the centralisation down to Motherwell, some people lived very near Eastfield depot ... lived there and worked there all their lives, travelling out to Motherwell was just ... not an option and so they took passenger jobs in Queen Street which were not the same thing. Anyway, so I had a bit of debate with myself about whether to take the passenger job really because ... although I'd only been doing the freight job a few months, there were a lot of things that were very ... there was a sense of achievement I suppose ... it was a more physical job and if everything was working okay ... even when everything wasn't working all right you still kind of knew what was going on and you weren't dealing with tickets or money or anything so ... it felt more like, it felt like a more operational job. That's probably what I quite liked about it and then in the train driving it was [a] completely different job but again it felt more kind of operational to do than obviously working doing revenue protection duties all the time which ... I wasn't so keen on ... doing the passenger guard's job and ... as you [had to be] confident that you had the necessary railway information to help the passengers. I think that's what frustrated the passenger guards the most, was when we didn't get the right information from control or wherever to pass on to people and you can just, you know, really feel the desperation of the passengers when everything's gone wrong or they – nobody's given them the right information – and you're not able to sort it yourself, or even give them the right information because you've not been given it either, you know? So, that got worse as the industry changed, I'll say that got worse with more people involved in trying to run the service and less people knowing what was actually going on ... I've met some very exasperated guards in the last couple of years.

TALES FROM THE MANAGEMENT

CATHERINE GREGORY ✦ 1987 AND 1990

A member of railway management recalls two very difficult situations

WHEN I WAS at Lincoln we had a passenger train derailment in the summer of '87 ... where we'd had some very hot weather ... it was a Sunday and essentially we'd had a track buckle because of the heat and the HST [High Speed Train] – which was still running at that time between Cleethorpes and London

– became derailed ... thankfully nobody was hurt, apart from ... scratches and bruises, and I was pretty much first on the scene.

I beat the area inspector because I just happened to be going out for a drink and we were at a pub which is next to a signal box and just as I'm sitting down with my glass of lager a signalman flings the window open and says, 'The HST's off the road at North Kelsey' so I had to leave the glass of lager and [go] straight back home and change ... as I say, I was first on the scene and stopping at the bridge just [by] the rear of the train and looking at it, you know, it was off the road and it was sort of slightly lifted up and the carriages ... weren't bent in themselves, but obviously the couplings between the connections were, had taken the strain and you just thought, 'Oh my goodness I hope nobody's hurt'...

[It] was a really strange thing getting there and what I'd realised about an incident, as we call them on the railway, is that you can't control people. You know the way it looks when you read the Rule Book and it tells you in General Appendix how you deal with things, you know it all feels as if it's going to be very orderly and you're going to be able to take people's names and you're going to, but then they all start piling off the train without ladders you know, obviously they want to get off, they want to get somewhere safe, they're milling about, they don't stay in the same place, you don't know who you've spoken to and its complete chaos and I hadn't really realised that but I mean we managed to get people dealt with. The police were already there when I'd got there and various other railway managers from adjacent areas sort of poled in during the afternoon and fortunately it was light, it was good weather, I mean that was the cause of the problem and there was a house nearby where people could just sort of sit down ... fortunately nobody was hurt but it was just the kind of complete chaos of everybody milling about that really still strikes me that it's so difficult to make sure everybody ... was there and you've got details 'cos people start making their own arrangements and you know arranging for taxis to come and all this sort of, you know, it's just ... very difficult to keep control of the whole situation 'cos you've got no kind of holding area, people start walking.

In December 1990 ... we managed to get the station at Sheffield completely flooded. I mean, when I say we, nobody actually on the railway caused this, but what happened was that ... the river actually flows underneath the station and there's a kind of barrage just at the back of the railway buildings, where ... there's a kind of mesh sort of fence that blocks everything from going down under there, so that any bits of logs or trees or any old debris that's got thrown in there, it actually stops any of that rubbish going under and blocking the free flow of the water under the station. Well for some reason although it had been raining very heavily and there'd been a lot of water moving through, whoever was responsible for actually ensuring that this, this sort of mesh was in the right position had failed to do so and as a result of which the ... river way under the station became very badly blocked and ... the water just came up and up and up and up and it was absolutely extraordinary ... I was called at home I think at about half seven in the morning because there had been a landslip in Totley Tunnel which was a wet tunnel ... but there had been a landslip and there were problems so, although I as Area Manager wasn't actually on call in terms of going to incidents to attend as first line, you were always on call as sort of second or third line, so I decided that ... I really ought to get myself across 'cos this looked as if it could turn into something quite serious, but by the time I got there ... I was there about nine o'clock I think and the emphasis had changed completely by the time I got into the control, from being concerned about this landslip in Totley Tunnel to being concerned about the rising level of water outside the station, which just rose and rose and rose and I still have photographs of cars outside Sheaf House ... the Sheffield Area Managers offices almost completely submerged by the rising tide of water. And it just rained and rained and sadly this was the weekend before Christmas and so there was a lot of people wanting to get to different places and I mean it was absolute chaos on that morning I have to say...

We had the control at York ringing up saying, 'Do you realise you have trains ... standing for two hours,' and you know all we could say is, 'Well you know if you can tell us how we're going to get them through this water that's absolutely fine, but if you can't they are going to have to stand a bit longer.' The whole of the station area was submerged and ... there was a kind of small team of us working ... in different shifts over ... the best part of a week, and the first day ... one of the first things that went was the generator in Sheaf House ... I think on the Sunday night ... there were three of us – the operations manager of course had just gone on his Christmas holiday abroad so he'd gone, so there was ... the assistant ops manager, myself and the passenger manager sitting round a candle in Sheaf House in the cold, 'cos there was no heat no light, and basically trying to work out how we going to replace 96 pairs of points that had all been completely ruined by the water, 'cos of course the water receded as soon as it stopped raining and as soon as the blockage was removed ... but ... you couldn't operate anything electrically, everything had to be renewed, so it was a case of very, very gradually over the next few days being able to take trains through the station essentially almost one at a time, and of course it made you realise what an incredibly busy station Sheffield was ... we put out a very detailed circular as to what was happening to trains...

It actually lasted into the New Year because ... we actually cleaned out all the Crewe Works back stock of points ... it was like re-signalling [the station] almost, you just needed everything they had we got and it was just a question of waiting till the next sets were manufactured, it was incredible really … that was really … the biggest and most problematic operational incident I've ever had to deal with … a huge problem for people who were trying to travel on the day … it's [the] Saturday before Christmas, not a good time for this to happen.

CHANGING TRACK

BRIAN DRUCE ✦ 1990s

A British Railways signalman, who joined the railways late in life, reflects on the changes he witnessed in the industry

I DIDN'T ACTUALLY JOIN the railways until my late 50s, which surprised quite a lot of people, but I was told they were examining the age profile of their signalmen, thinking that they could get rid of us in a few years' time because all the semaphore boxes would have gone, so I was not alone in being taken on a bit late in life. …

I went off in the early '80s to do a bit of work as a travelling ticket inspector on the Severn Valley Railway, and after a year of that I did the signalling course and qualified … I was lucky enough to be taken on at the end of 1990 … They sent me to Evesham, which was quite an interesting box…

And one day working the box, I noticed 600 yards away, by my home signal, what appeared to be a flock of crows or rooks on the line. I could see a lot of black dots on the ballast and in later years I always took binoculars to the box with me because my eyesight wasn't brilliant and it does help you to see the back of the dummy signal, to see whether it's cleared or not, and that sort of thing. So, I trained my binoculars on this flock of crows, it wasn't a flock of crows at all, it was a flock of sheep and of course, their wool was exactly the same colour as the ballast and the black I was seeing which I thought were birds were the sheep's heads. So, there's this vast number of sheep, just milling about and it was on the curve, by the home signal, so there was one of the London HSTs coming up, and luckily ... I was able to stop him at Bruern ... and said, 'Driver there's a lot of sheep on the line by my home signal, you'll keep a sharp look out and be prepared to stop short of the obstruction etcetera,' as we were supposed to do, which he did, and he hooted, and he moved very slowly and the sheep would not move to either side or both sides, he just drove them down the line towards me at a steady about three miles an hour, and just opposite the box there, there was a gap in the hedge and they were able to go into a field.

On another occasion, I had an HST held up in the platform because it had run out of fuel virtually and the driver said he pointed this out at London and his supervisor said, 'We don't care whether it's low on fuel, just take the train out.' And so I was on the phone to Swindon and all over the place and apart from the gauge in the cab ... and on the tank, there's some third method I think, you can check the fuel exactly, there was hardly anything there. The driver pleaded with me to be allowed to go on to Worcester, and I wouldn't let him because the last thing I wanted was an HST with perhaps a hundred people stuck on the single line between me and Norton Junction. So, he came up the box with his guard ... so they had to sit and wait, the passengers were taken on by a following Turbo, so they weren't delayed too badly. I had to stop on a bit late. It took four hours for a Class 47 assisting engine to come up from Bristol Bath Road. By now, my boss had come into the box and everything was happening and we were clipping points and things and up he came and he got on the phone at the home signal, of course because I couldn't clear it and I said, 'Right driver, you come in

[the] wrong road and hook on to the front of this failed HST.' I said, 'The points, the points are clipped.' The driver said to me, 'And scotched?' And my boss said, 'Clever clogs.' So I said to him, 'Yes.' And eventually it towed out this fuel-less train, but that couldn't happen now, of course because Bristol Bath Road has been closed, in the wisdom of the authorities, so where they get an engine from now, I have no idea. They might be able to get one from Saltley perhaps. But that illustrates the terrific change I think that has taken place in the way of there being spare staff and locos and carriage sets available. It's virtually ceased to be.

Let me tell you a little bit about how privatisation affected me and the railway. In the space of about five and a half years, which was all that my service was, there was an awful lot packed in, and in the course of that time, I worked for four different companies, doing exactly the same job. I started off with British Railways Western Region, after that I was working for Regional Railways Midland, then I was working for Railtrack Midland, and then I was working for Railtrack Great Western, with whom I finished. And this time of privatisation, I think was a great trauma for most of the employees. We'd already been through Organising for Quality ... we were subjected to all these things and we felt that they weren't really helping us to do our job properly; they weren't actually literally interfering with our work, but they weren't making it any easier. And, I think it was a fairly difficult time, but we came through it, and I remember, I think it was '94 when it all started. I was working in Moreton box and a nice youngish man came in, who was some gaffer from Birmingham, and he presented me with my Railtrack mug ... with some slogan on it about, about Railtrack, and I was supposed to be, to feel very pleased, I think, that I'd been presented with this mug, but I've still got it and I use it. And he said he was a bit sad because he'd been on the railway for

22 years or whatever it was and now he was going to become part of this privatised organisation, and so I asked him what his job was going to be, and he said he was going to be Production Manager. And I said, 'Well, we're running railways, what are you going to produce?' And he said, he had to think about this, 'I'm going to produce as many lucrative train paths as I can,' he said. That was his answer.

So those were the sort of things at which the old railwaymen would probably have been turning in their graves at, but there it was, and we got through it as best we could. The rationalisation, the reduction of staff, the doing away of the old-fashioned signal box, I felt, and a lot of people do, that there was great value in having a number of signal boxes, because in a sense they shepherded the trains along the rails, and there was someone to keep an eye on them. Everything now is getting so impersonal that something can go wrong and nobody might spot it for quite a while. You've no longer got the guard at the end of a goods train or a freight train. You haven't got the signal boxes every couple of miles, but in the Worcester area, we were lucky if we liked working manual boxes, as I did. We've still got about ten of them, and if management had had their way and the money, and the will, they'd have all gone … but there they are with a lot of very old, sometimes rather worn out equipment, and the technicians are always keeping busy to make sure everything is going properly. So that was something about privatisation and I thought it was rather sad, that once we had one great big railway which everybody was working for, and was more partnership and teamwork. Now there are 90 something different companies, and co-operation and communication is often not what it should be, in my opinion, and that is putting it politely.

Let me tell you about another box I did, this was all part of this rationalisation and privatisation business and my boss was keen to get things reorganised, because that was his remit,

I suppose, [to] do away with all these wonderful Spanish practices, as the press called them, or Byzantine practices, such as walking time. I could clock up hours of walking time, which all went back to the historical railway before signalmen had motor cars. They probably didn't even have bicycles and they had to walk to work, and if they were on the relief or whatever, they'd have to walk to a box miles away, and they were paid money for this. And this was still there within the system and the bosses naturally were very anxious to get rid of this, and it looked very bad and outmoded in the media. So he was keen, and they had a wonderful system, we needn't have relief signalmen any more, but by now we were becoming signallers, of course, because we had some ladies who'd joined us, which was very pleasant. They wanted to rationalise the signallers and they thought the relief people would no longer be necessary because each box would have enough signallers employed within it, on the shift system, so they'd never need to call in relief signallers, off the general roster. What they hadn't thought of course, was what if one of the signallers was on leave and another one or two of them went off sick, then somebody would have to be pulled in from outside. So this wonderful new system, it didn't last very long, but I was part of it and the boss was quite pleased to send me down to one of the Worcester boxes at Henwick, which is right in the city of Worcester there, and a very busy box indeed. At this time management were quite co-operative really, if you helped them, by fitting in with their scheme of things, and this particular boss, I remember, I mean, like most of them, they left you alone, which was nice because it was good to be independent in your box.

So I went down to Henwick Road, which is a junction and it's got a very, very busy road crossing with four barriers and as far as the railway layout was concerned, it was double track ... going away to Newland East in the down direction and coming up there was a double cross-over and there was also a siding and at the cross-over the line, the double line, separated into two single lines ... both which went through Foregate Street Station; one went round to Shrub Hill and up to Oxford and Gloucester and the other one turned left and went past Tunnel Junction box towards Droitwich and Birmingham. And these two single lines were worked by the acceptance lever system, which was yet another one for me to learn. I think I learned about half a dozen different methods of signalling in my short time. This box was very, very busy and it was quite true, you didn't have time to sit down and eat a meal, you were probably eating on the hoof. The only quiet times we had in the morning, were between ... quarter to seven and seven, that was quiet, we sent two trains in to Foregate and they were waiting to go at seven o'clock. So that was your time to visit the loo, which was a brick construction about 35 yards away down the yard, or make your cup of tea or glance at the paper, or whatever. The only other empty time as it were, was round about ten in the morning, when you had about ten or 15 minutes with nothing happening, but in that box the bells were always ringing, the phone was going ... And I remember one very hot summer afternoon in 1995, I think it was, there was a heat wave, the temperature in the box was about 90 Fahrenheit, even with all the windows open. I know under the Factory Acts, places of work should not go below a certain temperature, I don't know whether there's a regulation about the maximum. On that afternoon turn, I lost three pounds in weight, and I was working in my shorts and I had a shirt on and in between trains I sometimes took this, the shirt, off to try and, and cool down. So that was quite horrendous and one or two of the levers were pretty heavy and we had the barriers as well. Now, I'm quite sure that 99% of the public who came by and grumbled about being held up in their cars thought that all I was doing, and my colleagues were doing, was sitting in a nice armchair, and every time a train came along, pressed a button for the barriers, and then went back to my armchair again, and I think most of the public have no idea what happens in a signal box, until they visit one.

One of the best things I'd learnt, when I joined the railway, was that there was still a lot of teamwork. It was still one railway, it was British Railways Western Region and as in old style industries whether it was down the pits, or on farms or whatever, there was a lot of teamwork and even if you didn't like people, you still had to get on with them to the extent that you had to do the job together, and of course, there were a few oddballs and one or two awkward ones. There was one particularly awkward signalman, who delighted in confusing the younger men especially, and I think there were one or two drivers who seemed to believe that when they were on their way to work in the morning, they'd be thinking, 'How can I annoy a signalman today?' Or, 'Which signalman shall I annoy today?' And they would delight in pulling up at the box or reporting from a signal post telephone that one of your lamps was out or something was out of order or there was a gate open that sort of thing. Some of the drivers would stop and close the gate themselves, but not so, not so these two, and it seemed that they would try and make life for us as awkward as possible. In a sense I think there has always been rivalry between signalmen and drivers. One of the chaps who taught me the box said, 'Well, in the old days, if there was a controversy, it was always three against one, it was the driver, the fireman and the guard who all ganged up against the signalman.' And I believe in the old days the drivers would shout as they passed the box, as they'd been held up, 'Get the roof off.' Which meant 'let some air into the place and keep the signalman awake', and drivers would say that very often when they came on the phone to the signal box because they'd been held up at a red, the moment they picked the phone up, the signal changed to green and they thought that was evidence that the signalman had been asleep, and the moment he heard the phone ring from the signal post telephone, he immediately cleared the signal. Whereas often it wasn't the case, because at that very moment the driver picked the phone up, you'd just got line clear yourself, and went to clear the signal. But that was a bit about the sort of rivalry that existed, but mostly it was really very good teamwork and people were pretty friendly and there was a lot of social chat, when we had the time, and railwaymen are great raconteurs and get together with a pint or two and they will talk for hours because you were all part of the common thing, it wasn't the individualism that we've got today in society. So, we tended to get on quite well because we had to, and you relied on each other, and a lot of it was because public safety was involved. It wasn't a matter of choice, you were responsible for the safety of the trains.

One of the strange things, as one of the old signalmen pointed out to me, was that you could work next to a man, somebody in the next box a few miles away, for say ten years and you'd never actually meet him. You'd only ever speak to him on the telephone, but you built up a good relationship nevertheless. At my first box, because it was single-line working, we had to go out to the drivers and exchange tokens with them, I got to know all the Worcester drivers, all the ones that signed the road up to Oxford. Of course, not so many years ago, they used to go all the way to London, but things changed and their routes were cut back, so most of them came up to Oxford and back and there was usually the time for a few seconds of chat and pleasantries while we were changing tokens and this was good because it got you out of the box and you actually met another human being, otherwise you were stuck there for your eight hours, sometimes ten or twelve hours, and you might not see another soul for the entire length of that time, and because of that, I think a lot of signallers got the reputation for being a little bit weird, if you like because they were on their own so long. Although they were part of a team in one way, they were individuals in another and they didn't relate to other human beings often enough on the front, face to face basis, but generally in the old days, they had a very good social life ... at home they had their allotment, they had the pub and the darts and all the rest of it.

In those days we had quite a good relationship with the booking clerks, for example, and if the HST was going to be late and a lot of commuters hanging about for it, I'd ring up, I'd ring up my mate in the booking office and say, 'Ken, the London's about sixteen minutes late at Malvern, will you tell them?' And what we did, we cheated slightly, we used to say, 'The London is about ten minutes late.' It didn't sound quite so bad and it might make up a bit of time, so that was a bit of unofficial PR, I suppose, and we'd keep in touch on operational matters, and when things were quiet, we'd have a bit of a chat, and sometimes a grumble about things, but now things have changed and the booking clerks often don't know who's in the signal box, and they never speak on the phone and because they're not part of railway operations, but they're retail clerks, in some places they're not even supposed to go out on to the platform, and certainly in no way must they have anything to do with the track. I mean, at one time if a lady's handkerchief or something fell on to the track, they would jump down and pick it up, as a true gentleman. Or in those days if one of my signals was stuck, maybe in the off position and it wouldn't go back and ... I couldn't do it by pulling on the wire, it needed somebody to go out there and kick the counter balance weight or whatever and the signal was four or five hundred yards from my box, but it was only sixty yards from the booking office, I'd ring him up and he'd nip out and do it for me; that can't be done any more, that's all changed because you see, we're all different, we're all different bits of railway now.

SOURCES

EARLY STEAM

p.16   Samuel Smiles, *The Life of George Stephenson, Railway Engineer*, London, John Murray, 1857.

p.16   Fanny Kemble, *Records of a Girlhood*, Henry Holt and Company, New York, 1880.

p.22   Ibid.

p.25   Anon, 'Early railway travelling', Richard Pike (ed.), *Railway Adventures and Anecdotes: extending over more than fifty years*, London, 1884, pp.63–5.

p.27   Rev. Cookesley, 'Evidence on the Great Western Railway Bill', S C Brees, *Railway Practice*, London, 1838/9, p.252.

p.28   Joseph Hull, 'Evidence on the Great Western Railway Bill', S C Brees, *Railway Practice*, London, 1838/9, p.260.

p.30   Edward Sherwood, 'Evidence on the Great Western Railway Bill', S.C. Brees, *Railway Practice*, London, 1838/9, p.261.

p.31   W Meade Warner, 'Evidence on the London & Birmingham Bill', S C Brees, *Railway Practice*, London, 1838/9, pp.44–5.

p.33   Oliver Mason, 'Evidence on the London & Birmingham Bill', S C Brees, *Railway Practice*, London, 1838/9, pp.48–50.

p.34   Anon., 'A week at Manchester', *Blackwood's Edinburgh Magazine*, April 1839, pp.481–4.

p.40   *The Prose Works of William Wordsworth in three volumes*, Edward Moxon, Son, and Co., London, 1876.

p.47   Ibid.

p.52   Charlotte Brontë, Extract from letter to her father, 9 June 1851, Clement Shorter (ed.), *The Brontës' Life and Letters*, London, 1907.

p.53   M Saul, The Great Exhibition: letter to the Editor, *Preston Chronicle*, 18 June 1851.

p.55   Anon., Railway fares: letter to the Editor, *York Herald*, 28 June 1851.

SOURCES

GROWTH AND EXPLORATION

p.58　Anon., 'My Heart's in the Highlands', *All the Year Round*, 30 December 1865, pp.541–5.

p.61　Anon., 'No communication', *All the Year Round*, 7 November 1868, pp.522–3.

p.65　'T R', 'Tales of the MS&L: how we put on the Kybosh', *Great Central Railway Journal*, June 1918.

p.67　Anon., 'One day in Blackpool', *The Sphinx*, 22 July 1871, pp.229–31.

p.71　'T R', 'Tales of the MS&L: A queer finding', *Great Central Railway Journal*, February 1916.

p.74　Anon., 'Trip on an incline', *Chambers's Journal of Popular Literature, Science and Arts*, 13 February 1875, pp.100–1.

p.79　Clement Edwards, 'The shunter: a chapter from real life', *The Pall Mall Magazine*, December 1906, p.16.

p.81　Rev. V L Whitechurch, 'A trip on the footplate', *Good Words*, 1899, pp.91–3.

p.87　Anon., 'An engine driver's rewards', *London Journal*, 29 September 1900.

p.89　Wilfred Wemley, 'Driving on the broad gauge (How the other half lives: the engine driver)', *The English Illustrated Magazine*, July 1896, pp.341–6.

p.90　Ibid.

p.92　Alfred T Story, Engine drivers and their work, *The Strand Magazine*, July 1894, pp.279–87.

p.95　Ibid.

p.97　Anon., 'Some daring escapes from locomotives, told by a driver', *The London Journal*, 30 July 1910, p.329.

SIGNIFICANT EVENTS

p.102　Wynne Jackson, *Wynne's Diary: the life and times of an Edwardian lady*, at www.wynnesdiary.com.

p.104　Major A C Chauncy (writing as 'Julian Kaye'), 'Notes and Impressions IV', *Great Eastern Railway Magazine*, January 1915.

p.106 C J Hutcherson, 'Joining Kitchener's Army', *Great Eastern Railway Magazine*, November 1914.

p.108 Alfred Williams, *Life in a Railway Factory*, Duckworth and Co., London, 1915.

p.112 Major A C Chauncy (writing as 'Julian Kaye'), 'Notes and Impressions V', *Great Eastern Railway Magazine*, March 1915.

p.115 Anon., 'What life means to me: by a railway-guard of twenty-five years' experience', *Quiver*, May 1923, pp.692–4.

p.119 Anon., 'The return of the wanderer', *Furness & West Cumberland Railway Magazine*, October 1923, pp.87–8.

p.121 J D Bramley and A R Gamble (eds.), *Visions Afar: The journal of R W Carr, 1905–2005*, Sherburn, 2007, pp.158–9.

p.123 London School of Economics and Political Science Archives, London, Coll. Misc 760, Dover Dockers, Henry Duckworth diary entry, May 1926.

p.124 Lawrie Inman, Poppleton History Society oral history project interview.

p.127 Anonymous poem from the collection of Julian Holland.

p.128 An Assistant District Canvasser, 'On the Road', *London & North Eastern Railway Magazine*, December 1940, p.351.

p.131 Charles Day, interview recorded by John Vessey, 24 May 2001, York. Tape NAROH 2001-75, National Archive of Railway Oral History, National Railway Museum, York.

p.133 Anon., 'Carrying on', *London & North Eastern Railway Magazine*, October 1940, p.299.

p.136 William Squibb, interview recorded by Ian Gardiner, 11 July 2000, York. Tape NAROH 2000-31, National Archive of Railway Oral History, National Railway Museum, York.

p.139 Violet Lee, interview recorded by Ian Gardiner, 24 August 2000, York. Tape NAROH 2001-51, National Archive of Railway Oral History, National Railway Museum, York.

p.142 EP/EVAC, 'Evacuation Train Working', *London & North Eastern Railway Magazine*, July 1941, pp.174–5.

p.145 A Company Commander (London), 'The watch on the line', *London & North Eastern Railway Magazine*, February 1941, p.36.

SOURCES

p.148 Betty Chalmers, interview recorded by Frank Paterson, 8 August 2000, York. Tape NAROH 2000-40, National Archive of Railway Oral History, National Railway Museum, York.

p.150 Brian Palfreyman, interview recorded by John Vessey, 13 November 2000, York. Tape NAROH 2000-86, National Archive of Railway Oral History, National Railway Museum.

p.151 Sidney Sheldrick, interview recorded by Lew Adams, 14 June 2000, York. Tape NAROH 2000-18, National Archive of Railway Oral History, National Railway Museum, York.

THE END OF AN ERA

p.156 Stan Knowles, Poppleton History Society oral history project interview.

p.159 Talyllyn Railway Archives.

p.160 John Woodall, Poppleton History Society oral history project interview.

p.165 Ron White interviewed by Julian Holland.

p.167 Mohammed Ayub, interview recorded by John Vessey, 16 January 2003, York. Tape NAROH 2003-07, National Archive of Railway Oral History, National Railway Museum, York.

p.170 David Crew, interview recorded by John Vessey, 30 May 2000, York. Tape NAROH 2000-22, National Archive of Railway Oral History, National Railway Museum, York.

p.172 Brian Connorton, interview recorded by John Vessey, 23 November 2001, York. Tape NAROH 2001-179, National Archive of Railway Oral History, National Railway Museum.

p.174 Dick Smith, Poppleton History Society oral history project interview.

p.176 Charles Cook, interview recorded by Frank Paterson, 18 May 2000, York. Tape NAROH 2000-13, National Archive of Railway Oral History, National Railway Museum, York.

p.180 Stewart Currie, interview recorded by Frank Paterson, 17 April 2000, York. Tape NAROH 2000-02, National Archive of Railway Oral History, National Railway Museum, York

NEW BEGINNINGS

ACKNOWLEDGEMENTS

Julian Holland would like to thank the following organisations and people for their help in compiling this book:

Dr Susan Major for her tireless and extensive research.

Special thanks to Ed Bartholomew, Senior Curator, Image and Sound Collections, National Railway Museum, York for his work in tracing copyright clearance forms and providing permission to publish interviews with Charles Day, William Squibb, Violet Lee, Betty Chalmers, Brian Palfreyman, Sidney Sheldrick, Mohammed Ayub, David Crew, Brian Connorton, Charles Cook, Stewart Currie, Colin Mellish, Bill Addy, Geoff Page, Christine McMillan, Trevor Adams, Ann Henderson, Catherine Gregory and Brian Druce. The interviews were sourced from the National Archive of Railway Oral History (NAROH) at the National Railway Museum, York. Recordings were made between 2000 and 2002 as part of a volunteer project run by the Friends of the National Railway Museum and supported by the Heritage Lottery Fund. All the interviewers were volunteers.

Prudence Bebb, Chair, Poppleton History Society (PHS), together with Lawrie Inman, John Woodall, Stan Knowles and Dick Smith for permission to use extracts from PHS oral history interviews.

Don Bramley, for permission to use extracts from J D Bramley and A R Gamble (eds.), *Visions Afar: The Journal of R W Carr, 1905-2005*, Sherburn, 2007.

Richard Spendlove MBE, regional and local radio presenter and producer, and journalist Adrian Peel, for permission to use extracts from their interview (http://suite101.com/article/richard-spendlove-interview-a290080).

Peter Symes, grandson of Winifred Jackson (née Llewhellin), whose diary is transcribed and published by him at www.wynnesdiary.com.

The Talyllyn Railway and Don Newing, Archives Officer at the Talyllyn Railway Archives.

Jack Richards.

Bill King, Chairman, Great Eastern Railway Society, for information on 'Julian Kaye', the pseudonym of Major A C Chauncy.

John Drew, Project Leader, Dickens Journals Online at the University of Buckingham (www.djo.org.uk).

The following libraries:

Search Engine Library and Archive, National Railway Museum, York.

British Library, Boston Spa and St Pancras.

Borthwick Institute, University of York.

Robinson Library, Newcastle University.

York Minster Library.

City of York Archives and Local History collection.

Archive Services Group, Library, London School of Economics and Political Science.

And last, but certainly not least, David Eldridge and Holly Giblin at Two Associates for their work on the cover, Tracey Butler and Austin Taylor for typesetting, Alison Moore for proofreading and David Popey at AA Publishing for shaping the book into its final form.